Myths of Work

Myths of Work

The stereotypes and assumptions
holding your organization back

Ian MacRae and Adrian Furnham

KoganPage

First published in Great Britain and the United States in 2018 by Kogan Page Limited

2nd Floor, 45 Gee Street	c/o Martin P Hill Consulting	4737/23 Ansari Road
London	122 W 27th St, 10th Floor	Daryaganj
EC1V 3RS	New York, NY 10001	New Delhi 110002
United Kingdom	USA	India

www.koganpage.com

© Ian MacRae and Adrian Furnham, 2018

The right of Ian MacRae and Adrian Furnham to be identified as the authors of this work has been asserted by them in accordance with the Copyright, Designs and Patents Act 1988.

ISBN   978 0 7494 8128 5
E-ISBN 978 0 7494 8129 2

British Library Cataloguing-in-Publication Data

A CIP record for this book is available from the British Library.

Library of Congress Control Number

2017032051

Typeset by Integra Software Services, Pondicherry
Print production managed by Jellyfish
Printed and bound by CPI Group (UK) Ltd, Croydon, CR0 4YY

*To everyone with charisma, uniqueness,
nerve or talent. Bring it to work.*

CONTENTS

ACKNOWLEDGEMENTS

We would like to thank everyone who helped with this book or supported in its development in various different ways. Thanks to Karen Fox, Joe Parslow, Nicholas Parsons, Paul Rein and Heather Stewart for your help, with extra thanks to Zohra Ishan, who was extraordinarily helpful in putting this book together.

INTRODUCTION

Work and workplaces are in a state of flux. The nature and character of work has always been changing, but the pace of change seems to be accelerating, from younger people entering the workforce, to the growth in automation, computerization and changing relationships between employees and employers. There are many myths and preconceptions about work. Some of these myths hide grains of truth while others are entirely bogus.

Tackling these myths is a good opportunity to discuss the examples and evidence from workplaces and to debunk (or perhaps confirm) preconceptions and misconceptions about work. Confronting common myths of work is an ideal way to approach different ideas about work and workplaces because it allows us to approach it in a more irreverent, amusing and interesting way. Instead of spending hundreds of pages discussing obscure theories to lead up to one final point, we can skip those steps and launch directly into information and advice that is the most important and relevant to work.

Throughout this book we use stories, examples, case studies and humour to debunk or discuss common myths in the workplace. These are not designed to mock, ridicule or offend anyone but instead to highlight some of the sillier parts of some of the common myths of work. In the interest of good taste and impartiality, many of the least tasteful jokes within this book have been removed, along with anything mocking world leaders, or anything too offensive about disreputable public figures. The chapters are written to be entertaining and amusing while cutting swiftly through misapprehensions and misconceptions.

Each chapter is introduced as a myth. That is, something many or few people might believe about the workplace, how it operates or the people one might work with. These range from very commonplace myths that are quite easy to refute, like 'Millennials need a different working culture', to commonplace apprehensions about work that are much more likely to be true, such as 'A computer is going to take your job'. Although many of the chapters do discuss myths, stereotypes and misapprehensions, we find some of the chapters are imbued with a great deal of truth. Even as authors, researching some of these 'myths' revealed much more truth or surprising information about the workplace than we initially expected.

While each of the chapters confirms or refutes a myth and has a specific message, there is one important message that endures throughout this book. Whether the chapter is a myth or not, whether you agree or not, the best way to explore any of these workplace issues is to discuss them. We, as authors or as readers, can agree or disagree about a particular point. We can make amusing or sarcastic remarks about any of these points at work. We do, of course, discuss many serious, pressing and sometimes controversial issues. And it is as important to know the facts behind the issues or myths as it is to be able to discuss the topics in a respectful, enjoyable and interesting way.

These chapters should start the discussion, and the best way to make improvements in the workplace is to bring these discussions swiftly and directly into the workplace.

– MYTH 1 –

STAFF SHOULD WORK EIGHT-HOUR DAYS, MONDAY TO FRIDAY

Flexible working is here to stay for the foreseeable future – it is defined as the variation in working patterns where an individual can choose when their working day starts and ends and whether to work from home, the office or elsewhere.

Introduction

We've all learned how to go on Sunday night to e-mail and work from home. But very few of us have learned how to go to the movies on Monday afternoon. (Ricardo Semler, 2014)

Some people love their jobs. Some people watch the clock. The latter are perhaps more synonymous with those who describe their job as a simple 'nine to five'. The phrase nine to five is not a mere description of the number of hours an employee works but has taken on a greater cultural meaning. Having a nine-to-five job doesn't necessarily refer to someone who works from 9 am to 5 pm but symbolizes a person who has a full-time job that operates during standard business hours, Monday through Friday.

This traditional eight-hour shift was originated by Robert Owen in 1817, a social reformer who observed the long, gruelling 16-hour shifts that workers endured during the Industrial Revolution. He campaigned for the 40-hour week movement using the undisputable (at the time) logic that a balance in life is important. He proclaimed: 'Eight hours labour. Eight hours recreation. Eight hours rest.' Thus a 24-hour day should be split evenly between work, leisure and sleep.

It wasn't long before companies embraced the eight-hour day after seeing an increase in employees' productivity. The car company, Ford, was one of the first to take on the 40-hour week, with its competitors still remaining sceptical. However, after seeing the increase in Ford's profit margin (from US $30 million to US $60 million in two years) most followed suit. But is working eight hours a day, every day, Monday through Friday, really the most conducive to a productive environment, or are there other, more efficient ways of working?

The problems with an eight-hour work day

Profound technological changes have meant that the nature of work has drastically changed over a rapid amount of time. The internet, tablets and smartphones now make it possible for employees to work from anywhere at any time. No longer restricted to their cubicles or offices, workers have the ability to work remotely. It also means that those who work in an office can take their work home with them.

In the UK alone there is a rapidly rising number of employees who access their work e-mails at home: 81 per cent of office workers check their e-mail outside working hours, with a third of employees even checking their e-mails before they get out of bed in the morning (Guibourg, 2015). So realistically, a nine-to-five doesn't really exist as it's difficult to know how much extra time employees are working.

Time has become a way to measure productivity because it is perhaps the easiest way of doing so. However, in today's creative and mobile economy it is important to look towards other means of measurement. An eight-hour work day is not directly correlated to eight hours of productivity. An employee can sit at an office desk for eight hours but achieve very little, often being distracted by constant interruptions – a survey of 750 employees in 2014 reported that 31 per cent waste 30 minutes daily while 6 per cent waste over two hours daily at work (Conner, 2015). Employees are also diverse individuals; not everybody is productive at the same times. While some are early risers and work their best in the mornings, others are more inclined to work better during the night.

Is it working the number of hours a day that's the problem, or the rigidity of the workday? In 2000, France reduced its working hours from 39 to 35 hours a week, making it one of the shortest working weeks in the world. As an effort to increase job opportunities and work–life balance, Estevão and Sá (2008) examined the effectiveness of this policy change. They reported that France's law did not create more jobs and promoted behavioural changes that suggested that many workers were less happy with their working hours. Moreover, very few of France's white-collar workers actually work only 35 hours a week. Their suggestions for policy change are that the 35-hour workweek should be stopped and employees and firms should be free to choose the length of the workweek.

The future of working

Flexible working (also known as flexitime) is here to stay for the foreseeable future – it is defined as the variation in working patterns where an individual can choose when their working day starts and ends and whether to work from home, the office or elsewhere. There are great benefits to this way of working (Origo and Pagani, 2008). The measurable productivity benefits are real: Lloyds Banking Group reported that '66 per cent of line managers and colleagues considered that flexibility improved efficiency and productivity'. Greater flexibility also means an improved ability to meet clients and customer demands on a 24/7 schedule. Notably, employees who have more flexibility are more likely to be engaged and firms will have reduced turnover (Future of Work, 2012).

Millennials have already started throwing out the idea of a typical eight-hour workday. The Millennial Branding survey reported that 45 per cent of Millennials will choose workplace flexibility over pay (Schawbel, 2013). As more importance is placed on flexibility of working hours, freelancing has also become the new way of working. *Forbes* says that 34 per cent of the US workforce is now considered freelance, and this is set to rise to 40 per cent by 2020 (Taylor, 2013). The common reason behind this change in the nature of work is primarily the technological advancements that have occurred.

Generation 2020, who have grown up with these technologies, will start clocking on to these changes and embracing them themselves. At this very minute, these individuals are attending university and will soon enter the workforce, changing the way we work as we know it. They are well digitally connected, culturally liberal, extremely mobile and unwilling to settle for anything less. Not unlike some other groups of individuals…

There are some individuals who take flexible working to the next level; they are known as 'digital nomads'. Pieter Levels (2015) predicts that by 2035 there will be a billion digital nomads in the world. They take advantage of technological advancements and work remotely from wherever they want, more than likely running their businesses from a tropical island in the Caribbean. For example, Hubud is a co-working space that has opened in Bali, Indonesia and they believe they are the future of the workplace. Their tagline, 'co-working, co-living, co-learning and co-giving' has brought together a large group of fiercely independent individuals who are seeking to change the way they work.

Conclusion

Although a digital nomad's way of working may be extreme, and only suited to certain industries, organizations must look up from their traditional ways and learn to incorporate more flexible working hours, or risk losing out on recruiting new top talent (Kelliher and Anderson, 2008). The first step is to look at their organizational culture and their employee demands and needs and try and ensure they meet them.

References

Conner, C (2015) Wasting time at work: the epidemic continues, *Forbes*. Available at: https://www.forbes.com/sites/cherylsnappconner/2015/07/31/wasting-time-at-work-the-epidemic-continues/#1d9424901d94

Estevão, M and Sá, F (2008) The 35-hour workweek in France: straightjacket or welfare improvement? *Economic Policy*, **23** (55), pp 417–63

Future of Work (2012) The benefits of flexible working arrangements: a Future of Work Report. Available at: http://www.bc.edu/content/dam/files/centers/cwf/ individuals/pdf/benefitsCEOFlex.pdf

Guibourg, C (2015) Email addicts? One in three UK office workers check their work email in bed, *City AM*. Available at: http://www.cityam.com/223107/ email-addicts-one-three-uk-office-workers-check-their-work-email-bed

Kelliher, C and Anderson, D (2008) For better or for worse? An analysis of how flexible working practices influence employees' perceptions of job quality, *The International Journal of Human Resource Management*, **19** (3), pp 419–31

Levels, P (2015) The future of digital nomads: how remote work will transform the world in the next 20 years. Available at: https://levels.io/ future-of-digital-nomads

Origo, F and Pagani, L (2008) Workplace flexibility and job satisfaction: some evidence from Europe, *International Journal of Manpower*, **29** (6), pp 539–66

Semler, R (2014) How to run a company with (almost) no rules, *TED*. Available at: https://www.ted.com/talks/ricardo_semler_how_to_run_ a_company_with_almost_no_rules/transcript?language=en

Schawbel, D (2013) Millennial Branding and Beyond.com survey reveals the rising cost of hiring workers from the Millennial generation, *Millennial Branding*. Available at: http://millennialbranding.com/category/blog/page/4/

Taylor, K (2013) Why Millennials are ending the 9 to 5, *Forbes*, 23 August. Available at: https://www.forbes.com/sites/katetaylor/2013/08/23/ why-millennials-are-ending-the-9-to-5/#7db55841715d

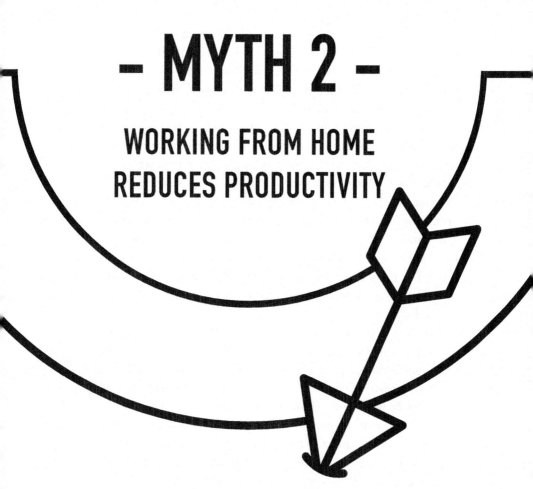

– MYTH 2 –

WORKING FROM HOME REDUCES PRODUCTIVITY

More than one-third of employees would take the opportunity to work from home over a pay rise.

Introduction

Work is becoming ever more flexible in where, how and when it can be completed. The prevalence and frequency of employees working from home are increasing (Chokshi, 2017). Some companies have even moved to completely flexible working conditions where employees have complete control over their own work schedule and are evaluated only on their productivity and output irrespective of hours worked (MacRae and Furnham, 2017).

However, there is an enduring myth that people need to be in a traditional office environment with standard models of direct supervision to be productive workers. Some believe that there are too many distractions in the home. Partners, roommates, children, diversions, hobbies and other entertainments may seem to be too nearby for the worker to focus on the job at hand. Indeed, some people have trouble working at home. It begs the question of whether or not employees should be able to work from home, and whether it is a more or less effective environment to work in.

These are important questions to ask about remote working because working from home is becoming increasingly commonplace. Those who do work remotely are doing more of their work remotely than ever before. The number of remote workers spending less than 20 per cent of their time working remotely fell from 34 per cent in 2012 to 25 per cent in 2016. The number of workers spending 80 per cent of their time working remotely increased from 24 per cent to 31 per cent in the same time period (Chokshi, 2017).

Research from Gallup polls in the United States shows that the flexibility to work from home and flexible scheduling are also becoming more and more important for job seekers. Many people want some control and flexibility over their work schedule. Some parents want more flexibility so their schedules fit better with those of their children. Others want to be able to take mornings or afternoons off, many people prefer to work the hours that suit them instead of a standard nine-to-five work day. The flexibility to work from home is so important to so many people that a study by Global Workplace Analytics found that more than one-third of employees would take the opportunity to work from home over a pay rise.

Working remotely certainly is becoming more common, and it is a trend that is likely to continue to increase in coming years. As an evolving phenomenon, it is impossible to predict all the effects, but there is certainly evidence to suggest flexible and remote working can improve productivity, reduce costs and improve the lot of workers.

Evidence for increased productivity

An experiment in remote working conducted by Stanford University and the University of Beijing tested the productivity of call centre workers who worked remotely compared with those who worked in their regular office (Bloom et al, 2015). When workers were randomly assigned to either work from home or in the office for a period of nine months, those who worked from home actually had 13 per cent higher performance than the office-assigned group. Those who worked from home had less sick leave and also attributed their increased effectiveness to a quieter work environment.

Although studies like that of Bloom and his colleagues with call centre workers are useful indicators that working from home can improve productivity, it should be noted there is no guarantee this effect will always be present across industries and jobs. Though other examples, such as in MacRae and Furnham (2017) show that flexible working arrangements can improve performance and employee satisfaction in highly skilled professional occupations, this is still a relatively new way of working, and it is impossible to draw firm conclusions for every industry or workplace.

Flexible work arrangements and working from home would appear to be good business decisions, both for workplace productivity and in offering attractive jobs to workers who want more independence and flexibility. Employers should not take this as advice to automatically give workers carte blanche in all of their activities. Employers would be wise to develop working arrangements that incorporate clear measures of performance that can be compared between on-site and off-site workers. Remote working is an opportunity that can be tried cautiously so its effects can be tested in the unique circumstances of each industry and company.

An example

In *Motivation and Performance: A guide to motivating a diverse workforce*, MacRae and Furnham (2017) provide a detailed case study of a company that turned improved workplace flexibility into greater productivity and profitability.

Ryan is a relatively new tax and accountancy services company that was founded in 1991. It grew rapidly from revenues of US $156,000 in its first year of operating to over US $400 million now. However, as the company grew in revenue, profitability and number of employees, the working conditions deteriorated. The workplace was described as a 'well-paid sweatshop' where employees had to work long and straining hours with very limited flexibility, vacation time and employee benefits. High employee turnover (about 20 per cent) was expensive and clearly linked to the sweatshop culture.

In 2008, they decided to move to a more flexible system – with complete flexibility for employees and teams. Instead of mandatory long hours that were demanded by the workplace culture, Ryan decided to measure performance based on the quality of employees rather than the amount of time they logged.

Along with better, rigorous methods of measuring performance, employees and teams were given discretion to determine their performance criteria, as well as how, when and where they worked. Employees could work from home on certain days or certain hours, take as much holiday time as they wanted (assuming they got their work done) and choose their working hours at their own discretion. Within a few years, this policy drastically reduced staff turnover, while employee headcount continued to increase. Employee engagement as well as productivity increased remarkably. For further details about this example, see MacRae and Furnham (2017).

Cost saving

The savings companies can make when employees work from home are immediately apparent. *Entrepreneur* magazine reports that employees who work from home just half of the time save their company about US $11,000 per year. Employees who are not in the office use fewer of the company resources, occupy less physical space and don't incur various other expenses related to being on-site. It also cuts the transportation costs of those employees getting to and from the office (Hendricks, 2014).

Having more engaged, satisfied employees also comes with decreased turnover and reduced costs associated with stress and sick days. Employees who work from home also tend to be healthier, from taking fewer sick days to reporting healthier eating habits and having a better work–life balance. All of this translates into employees who are more loyal to the company, less likely to leave, and consequently save the company money.

Loss of community and social environment

Does moving offsite make work lonelier and more isolating? It may seem that chats with colleagues, shared lunches or drinks after work may be lost when everyone chooses to work from home instead of going into a shared office space. Much of the speculation on telecommuting guessed that remote working would make workers feel isolated

However, this too is changing. In 2012, when workers were surveyed about when they felt most engaged in their work, the workers who spent most time on-site at work (at the physical location) reported the highest levels of engagement. But by 2016, the workers who spent three to four days working off-site reported the highest rates of engagement. Despite spending the majority of their time remotely, these workers still reported that people at work cared about them, were supportive of their development and talked to them about their progress. The days of the remote worker being socially isolated seem to be fast disappearing.

A surprising finding about remote working was that it actually left the remaining office workers who chose *not* to move off-site feeling isolated. Research by Kevin Rockmann and Michael Pratt (2015) found that the negative social effects of remote working were felt most by those who chose to remain working at the office. Of the remaining office workers, many came into the physical office location to get a sense of community and for the social interaction offered in the physical office space. When many of their colleagues left to work on their own schedules, the remaining workers felt disconnected and socially isolated from the overall group. Instead of being an energizing, inspiring workplace, 'the office essentially became an isolated wasteland', said Rockmann.

His research of Fortune 100 tech companies in Silicon Valley found that the decision to work from home rapidly became contagious and many workers were drawn to the possibility of setting their own schedule and working wherever they wanted. For this highly skilled workforce able to complete much of their work remotely, the draw was too much to resist. The consequences were unexpected, though. Teamwork fell sharply, and sponta-neous ideas generated through conversations in the office diminished, thus ultimately negatively affecting productivity levels.

The bigger picture

The benefits of working remotely seem to be great, with the evidence point-ing to remote working as a promising way of improving productivity and performance of workers while simultaneously reducing costs.

But working from home is not for everyone. Some workers are motivated by the social interactions, the conversations and the community around them in an office. Some people work much better in a traditional office space where they have a manager supervising their work, and where there are fewer distractions than they would encounter at home.

Much of the current research on remote working focuses on relatively highly skilled professions or types of work that can be done on one's own. We cannot assume that the productivity gains from working remotely that have been seen in some occupations will necessarily translate into other types of work. And many types of work need a physical presence. From hair stylists to car mechanics, some work cannot just be outsourced or moved offsite.

There are also potential consequences to moving remote working that are impossible to foresee. How fractured will companies and teams become if every employee moves offsite and workplaces no longer have a shared, physical space? There are some indications that the consequences of this could be severe, but the honest answer is we don't yet know the long-term effects of remote working, particularly if and when it becomes the predominant mode of work. The benefits seem very promising, but progress should be made with caution. There may be unpredictable consequences.

Conclusion

Working from home may not be for everyone. It is certainly a myth that working from home reduces productivity. The evidence clearly shows that remote workers are more satisfied, more productive and even healthier than the lonely on-site colleagues left in the traditional office.

However, there's still a great deal to learn about the effects of working remotely. Not everyone is able to be self-motivated and work independently from home. These individuals may need more supervision and encouragement from remote managers, or may just be more productive in a traditional office environment. The traditional office should not be completely scrapped just yet – but it could be reimagined and redesigned to be more effective today and in the future.

References

Bloom, N et al (2015) Does working from home work? Evidence from a Chinese experiment, *The Quarterly Journal of Economics*, 130 (1), pp 165–218

Chokshi, N (2017) Out of the office: more people are working remotely, survey finds, *New York Times*, 15 February. Available at: https://www.nytimes.com/2017/02/15/us/remote-workers-work-from-home.html

Global Workplace Analytics (nd) Advantages of agile working strategies for companies. Available at: http://globalworkplaceanalytics.com/resources/costs-benefits

Hendricks, D (2014) 5 Ways telecommuting saves employers' money, *Entrepreneur*, 14 July. Available at: https://www.entrepreneur.com/article/235285

MacRae, I and Furnham, A (2017) *Motivation and Performance: A guide to motivating a diverse workforce*, Kogan Page, London

Rockmann, K W and Pratt, M G (2015) Contagious offsite work and the lonely office: the unintended consequences of distributed work, *Academy of Management Discoveries*, 1 (2), pp 150–64

– MYTH 3 –

SOCIAL MEDIA SHOULD NEVER BE USED AT WORK

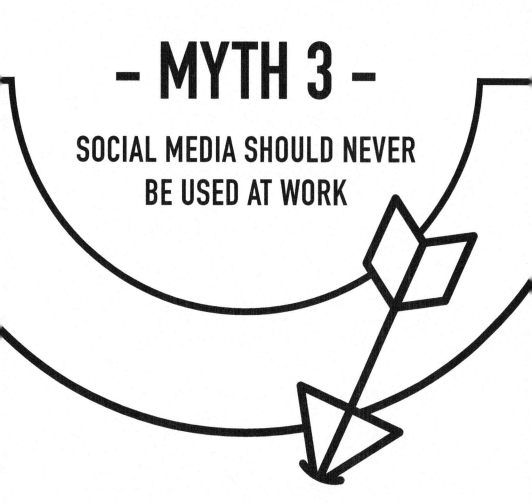

Despite the potential for social media to improve productivity in the workplace, the 72 per cent of companies that are using social media aren't utilizing it to its fullest potential.

Introduction

It's 2017 and everyone from young children to grandmothers is on some form of social media. Social media is the term used for internet-based tools used on computers, tablets, and smart phones to help people interact and share information, ideas and views. Given the vast array of social media sites and applications that exist, such as Twitter, Facebook and YouTube to name a few, it can be easy to conclude that they can only be a source of distraction, particularly at work. Yet contrary to popular belief, new academic research has proposed that 'workers who are encouraged to tweet, chat, like, and Skype on the job are among the most productive' (Warner, 2013).

We live in a social economy where our knowledge is currency (Meister, 2013). Millions of people organize large parts of their lives online and communicate using social media. Thus, as work is such a big part of our lives, it is only natural that some of it will filter into interactions online. And the faster we can make these interactions occur, the quicker we receive a greater amount of knowledge in work-related matters, subsequently having a large impact on productive capacity.

Research firm Future Workplace (Meister, 2013) conducted a survey of over 1,000 employees from a range of different companies. They highlighted that 60 per cent of Millennials and almost 80 per cent of Generation 2020 said that by the year 2020, social media literacy will be required of all employees in the workforce. Therefore, the changing demographics of the workforce mean that organizations may need to keep up with the changing nature of work and learn how to utilize it to their benefit.

The benefits of social media access

It sounds counterintuitive, but when employees are able to go online and use social media for a short while, their productivity levels rise, at least according to the academic experts. Subramaniam and his colleagues (2013) at Warwick business school have studied employees' social media use (including Skype, Facebook and an internal communication software) at a leading telecommunications company, MaxCom, at their offices in Finland, the UK and Germany. They found that increased digital connectivity within these firms allowed people to feel more empowered. This empowerment stemmed from greater flexibility of where and when they work that they gained from having access to social media.

Jobs are no longer a simple nine-to-five affair in the modern working world, so greater control over timing through social media has been reported to lead to more effective and efficient completion of tasks. Of course, there needs to be specific internal and external social media communication policies that specify where, how, when and why social media can and should be used in the workplace. It needs to be emphasized that social media and digital communication tools should be used for work-related purposes, not on personal or distracting pursuits.

Despite the potential for social media to improve productivity in the workplace, the 72 per cent of companies that are using social media aren't utilizing it to its fullest potential (McKinsey Global Institute, 2012). That's not to say that all social media is made equal, nor are all social media platforms designed for the same purposes. There is a difference between accessing a personal Facebook account to post pictures of kittens, and using an internal or external social media network to communicate work-related information with colleagues and clients. That is why it is so important to be focused, deliberate and well-informed about different social media platforms and their possible benefits at work. Internal company-focused social media platforms can be more useful for internal communication. Public-facing companies may find more public social media platforms like Facebook, Twitter and LinkedIn more useful for sharing marketing or communications information with a public audience.

Certain industries could raise productivity by 20 to 25 per cent if they used the full breadth of what social media offers. Firms that have 'interaction workers' (high-skill and knowledge workers), according to McKinsey, are likely to benefit the most. Using social media as an internal source of information that is accessible can reduce an employee's time spent searching for information by 35 per cent, time which can be used more productively. Think of what can be done with 35 per cent more time!

Even personal social media access can also increase productivity in the right circumstances. Pew Research Center (Olmstead, Lampe and Ellison, 2016) reported that 54 per cent of employees questioned said that using social media during their breaks helped them recharge at work. Social media breaks allow employees a form of escapism from their work days and has a subsequent positive impact on focused attention to tasks. As long as employees don't take 'social media breaks' every five minutes.

Another key finding from Subramaniam's study was that with more online interactions with co-workers and clients, the more knowledge was gained. Employees were able to keep up to date with new information and developments within their field. Fonality, a communications company, previously reported that workers waste an average of 67 minutes a day trying to find relevant information in an ineffective manner. However, the socially connected workers at companies such as MaxCom are able to overcome this issue and gather information quickly from online sources.

Social media access provides some new opportunities for information gathering (Salz, 2006). Research studies have found that employees will often use social software such as blogging, and social bookmarking tools to search and compile information within a corporate environment (Millen, Feinberg and Kerr, 2006). Thus, social media is not restricted to connecting and interacting with others but is also about the knowledge that can be gained.

The happiness and welfare of employees is also important to consider when companies set social media policies. Social media access can help to create a fun work atmosphere for employees. In return, happy employees are likely to work harder and give more back into the company.

When social media works best

Organizations who have blocked social media access typically do so to avoid productivity loss and protect against viruses or maintain privacy. These issues still remain if social media access is provided without boundaries – research has shown that internal social media systems tend to work best for a corporate environment. Millen, Geyer and Muller (2008) created an internal social networking software called 'Beehive' for the global company IBM. Each individual is given a profile and the ability to befriend colleagues like other social networking sites. An analysis of the use of this social media platform showed a positive impact on employee morale. Employees who initially signed up to interact with close friends at work ended up moving away from this and meeting new people instead and expanding their social networks. Some employees believed the site could help them move up in their careers by promoting themselves and connecting with others strategically.

Conclusion

In a 2016 survey from Pew Research Center, 77 per cent of over 2,000 American workers surveyed reported that, despite their employers' policies against social media use, they still used it anyway (Olmstead, Lampe and Ellison, 2016). And given that the next generation will most likely use social media platforms as their primary communication means, it is important for organizations to fully embrace social media and all its potential benefits including productivity rises and greater social networking opportunities. Firms who are more reluctant may benefit greatly from internal social software that minimizes the risks involved with employees' access to social media during the working day.

References

McKinsey Global Institute (2012) The social economy: unlocking value and productivity through social technologies. Available at: http://www.mckinsey.com/industries/high-tech/our-insights/the-social-economy

Meister, J (2013) The Boomer-Millennial workplace clash: is it real? *Forbes*. Available at: https://www.forbes.com/sites/jeannemeister/2013/06/04/the-boomer-millennial-workplace-clash-is-it-real/#e6475b323ca0

Millen, D R, Feinberg, J and Kerr, B (2006) Social bookmarking in the enterprise, *Social Computing*, 3 (9)

Millen, D R, Geyer, W and Muller, M (2008) *Motivations for Social Networking at Work*, IBM Research

Olmstead, K, Lampe, C and Ellison, N B (2016) Social media and the workplace, *Pew Research Centre*. Available at: http://www.pewinternet.org/2016/06/22/social-media-and-the-workplace

Salz, P A (2006) Social networking tools on the road to enlightenment, *EContent*. Available at: http://www.econtentmag.com/Articles/Editorial/Feature/Social-Networking-Tools-on-the-Road-to-Enlightenment-18109.htm

Subramaniam, N, Nandhakumar, J and Baptista, J (2013) Exploring social network interactions in enterprise systems: the role of virtual co-presence, *Information Systems Journal*, 23, pp 475–90

Warner, B (2013) When social media at work don't create productivity-killing distractions, *Bloomberg*. Available at: https://www.bloomberg.com/news/articles/2013-04-01/when-social-media-at-work-dont-create-productivity-killing-distractions

– MYTH 4 –

LISTENING TO MUSIC WHILE WORKING IS DISTRACTING

Treating employees like responsible adults often means giving them the freedom to make their own decisions about how they get their work done. If they prefer to listen to music while they work, it raises their mood or makes the job more enjoyable, surely they should be given that option.

Introduction

Psychologists have found all sorts of benefits that come from listening to music. At a party or social gathering for example, music can put people in a good mood, make them more sociable, get the conversation going and create more enjoyable experiences (Furnham and Bradley, 1997; Cassidy and MacDonald, 2007).

Many people enjoy listening to music to pass the time, for enjoyment or to block out other sounds. Mobile phones and portable music players have made it easy for almost everyone to listen to music anytime, anywhere. So should offices play music for employees? Should employees be able to block out the noise and distractions of their office environment by listening to their own music through headphones? Does it boost productivity, or serve as a distraction? Or is there any effect at all? From a management and productivity perspective, the question is about whether music is a help or a hindrance in the office environment. Some people believe that if someone has their headphones in at work, they are not paying attention to the task at hand.

The research on the topic provides a characteristically indefinite answer: it depends. Music preferences and tastes vary hugely, and have different emotional effects on different people. Music can induce a substantial range of different emotions from happiness and delight, to amusement, disgust, annoyance or sadness. This is why most workplaces or businesses that do play music tend to broadcast some generic and inoffensive popular music.

There is some evidence, at least, that workers like listening to music at work. Seventy-three per cent of workers in warehouses say that they are more productive when music is playing, and in a survey, 65 per cent of businesses believed that music made their workers more productive (Barford, 2013). But music can affect people very differently depending on the kind of music and the person.

Background noise

Generic, bland and inoffensive music is probably the safest choice for employers who do play music, or for businesses that play music for their customers. It avoids all the potential concerns about offending employees or customers, endorsing political views or other ideologies.

Unless there is a good reason to be playing music as generic background noise, it is not going to boost productivity. The research on general background noise is clear: it harms productivity. Background noise in general is a distraction at work, and the more challenging or intellectually demanding the work is, the more distracting background noise can be (Perham and Vizard, 2010; Cassidy and MacDonald, 2007). Simple, mundane or routine tasks like stocking shelves or sweeping floors aren't hugely affected. But work that involves things like reading complex information, writing reports or doing mathematical tasks can be significantly negatively impacted by background noise.

When music is essentially just insipid background noise it's not going to interfere too much with simple or routine tasks. However, for more complex or demanding tasks, background music can reduce productivity.

Types of music

The more complex question is that of music type and personal taste. Particularly in an office environment with a diverse workforce, it is likely that music tastes are very different. Hymns or religious music might be inappropriate to a general office environment, but completely appropriate in a cathedral. Death metal may be appropriate for a niche clothing company but would be less appropriate in a cathedral.

Music can be very distracting when it causes negative emotions. Songs that people find annoying, distressing or just generally of poor quality will distract from the work, reducing productivity, and likely putting people in a bad mood.

A popular psychology article in the *Telegraph* (Davidson, 2016) suggests that music improves productivity when the type of music fits with the task. For example, they suggest:

- classical music for work that involves detailed or complex numerical tasks;
- pop music for data entry and meeting looming deadlines;
- ambient music for solving equations;
- dance music for problem solving and proofreading.

The research is a bit questionable, and only included 26 participants, so the results should be taken with a pinch of salt. These specific music choices are unlikely be universally applicable. There is some truth to it though, because whether or not music has words can have a significant impact on productivity when the job involves writing. This is because the part of your brain that deals with language can be overwhelmed when you're listening to the words in the song and trying to write something completely different (Covarrubias, nd; Perham and Vizard, 2010).

Personal choice

Like any workplace policy, if it's poorly thought out it is likely to cause more harm than good. While there is evidence that music can improve employee mood and productivity, blaring Coldplay or Nickelback on repeat might have a counterproductive effect.

It is not surprising that music can improve productivity and mood amongst employees when they listen to the music *they like*. If employees are able to listen to music without disturbing others, and select the music of their choice, it may very well be beneficial. But it is still better suited to certain tasks, perhaps a good song lifting their mood while performing a boring, simple or repetitive task. If the work is more complex or demanding, silence or instrumental music might be better.

Another matter to consider in allowing employees to listen to music at work is the level of autonomy they are given. Employees in highly skilled, complex or challenging types of work should certainly have the choice and independence to listen to their own music (providing it doesn't disturb others and is not a safety concern).

Considering the bigger picture, treating employees like responsible adults often means giving them the freedom to make their own decisions about how they get their work done. If they prefer to listen to music while they work, it raises their mood or makes the job more enjoyable, surely they should be given that option.

Headphones and social distance?

The other matter to consider is the social effects of some or many employees wearing headphones at work throughout the day. One of the benefits of a co-working space is the opportunity for conversation, innovation and open communication amongst colleagues.

If the office becomes an environment where everyone uses music to isolate themselves in their own bubble, it could erode the social bonds within the office environment. If people choose to use music to filter out the entire office, it can create social distance even when people are physically close together. Music might be useful for focusing and filtering out distractions on a particular task, but if all employees listen to their own music it has the potential to reduce team productivity and cohesion.

Getting the balance is important. If you have intelligent, motivated and independent workers, they should be able to have some autonomy and independence in their working conditions. They should be encouraged to work privately and independently when efficiency is the highest priority. But music should not be used as a distraction when team cohesion and working together is the priority.

Conclusion

Music is highly personal. It certainly can be a distraction, particularly when completing demanding or complex tasks. But it can also lift the mood, filter out distractions and make the work environment better for employees. Ultimately it comes down to personal discretion, making sure the music (or lack of) fits the work environment and giving people the independence to listen to their own music when appropriate.

If you're unsure of the type of music to play though, by far the safest track will always be John Cage's 4'33". The piano version is particularly good.

References

Barford, V (2013) Does music in the workplace help or hinder? *BBC Magazine Monitor.* Available at: http://www.bbc.com/news/blogs-magazine-monitor-24017145

Cassidy, G and MacDonald, R A R (2007) The effect of background music and background noise on the task performance of introverts and extraverts, *Psychology of Music,* **35** (3), pp 517–37

Covarrubias, G (nd) To listen or not to listen: music vs productivity, HireDePaul. Available at: https://hiredepaul.org/2017/01/11/to-listen-or-not-to-listen-music-vs-productivity/

Davidson, L (2016) This is the kind of music you should listen to at work, *Telegraph,* 2 June. Available at: http://www.telegraph.co.uk/business/2016/06/02/this-is-the-kind-of-music-you-should-listen-to-at-work/

Furnham, A and Bradley, A (1997) Music while you work: The differential distraction of background music on the cognitive test performance of introverts and extraverts, *Applied Cognitive Psychology,* **11**, pp 445–55

Perham, N and Vizard, J (2010) Can preference for background music mediate the irrelevant sound effect? *Applied Cognitive Psychology,* **25** (4), pp 625–31

– MYTH 5 –

HEALTH AND SAFETY IS THE ENEMY

Health and safety is not just another form of political correctness, it's a way of making sure the business is resilient, prepared and runs effectively.

Introduction

Has health and safety 'gone mad'? Is the concept of health and safety some sort of attempt by a ballooning nanny state to control and stifle all business activities, depress productivity and bind employers up in administrative red tape and regulation? Or does it have at least some level of usefulness in the contemporary workplace?

Excessively heavy-handed and silly policies that invoke the name of health and safety are favorite tabloid fodder. Take *The Sun*'s headline: 'Couple's doormat seized after council staff deem it a health and safety risk – and the jobsworth charged them a £40 removal fee' (Pattinson, 2016). Or 'Elf and safety gone mad as Northern Ireland councils ban Santa from throwing sweets to children' (Black, 2016).

In fact, many of the sillier and more far-fetched rules imposed in the name of 'health and safety' have nothing to do with real health and safety regulations or the core purpose of making workplaces and businesses safer and avoiding compromising people's health. Judith Hackitt, chairman of the Health and Safety Executive says, 'We never cease to be amazed by the cases we consider. Why on earth do people think they can get away with banning pint glasses with handles, bubbles at a birthday party, or burgers served anything other than well done, claiming they are a health and safety hazard?' (Martin, 2013).

Well, it may have something to do with previous stories like 'Time is called on traditional pint glass after government brands them too dangerous' (Claire Bates in the *Daily Mail*, 2009), or 'Chefs ordered to cook meat patties only "well done" in food safety crackdown' (Sinead Maclaughlin in the *Daily Mail*, 2016).

A good rebuttal to some of the less constructive health and safety tabloid headlines was by Kevin Myers (2009), published in the *Daily Mirror*: 'We are as frustrated as most when organizations use "health and safety" as an excuse to avoid doing things, ban activities or spoil people's fun.' He goes on to acknowledge that the media can have a constructive role in highlighting some of the sillier as well as the more constructive health and safety rules. Having a public discussion about health and safety is a good way to make sure it is fit for purpose for businesses and employees.

The historical perspective on health and safety

Health and safety has been discussed in various ways in the workplace and in the media for a very long time. It is very helpful to look at the historical role and value of health and safety in the workplace to get a better sense of its real value.

The real purpose of health and safety is quite clear and simple: to prevent unnecessary accidents and illness at work, and avoid damaging people's health at work where possible. There's the ethical argument about not killing or maiming your employees or customers and not giving them deadly or harmful diseases that seems logical. But there's also a straightforward business case: accidents and injuries at work are expensive.

About 30 million working days are lost in the UK every year from workplace-related illness or injury (HSE, 2016) and workplace-related health and illness problems cost the UK economy about £14 billion per year while the US economy bears a cost of US $250 billion. That's about eight times as much as all the costs of cancer or more than three times the cost of diabetes (OSH, 2012). Around the developed world, estimates generally put the cost of workplace injury or illness of between 1 and 3 per cent of national GDP, varying by country (European Agency for Safety and Health at Work, 2013). That's a substantial cost.

Taking a historical perspective, health and safety has made a massive difference for workers. A great deal of progress has been made since the brutal working conditions of Victorian work houses and dangerous industrial and resource-extraction jobs of the 19th and early 20th centuries. Research from the United States (NSC, 1998) shows that work-related injuries fell about 90 per cent between the beginning and end of the 20th century. One hundred years ago, you were almost 10 times more likely to be killed on the job as you would be today.

This is of course influenced by the type of work and industries people are in. Yet even the industries where people are more likely to be injured or killed at work have massively reduced the risk of injury. Health and safety rules have been introduced to mitigate the very real risks to personal health that can occur in any workplace or type of job.

We see a similar picture in the UK, with the positive trend continuing to recent years. Workplace fatalities halved from 1995/96 to 2014/15 in the UK (HSE, 2015a). Fatal injuries have fallen to one-sixth of their rate in 1974, when the Health and Safety at Work Act was introduced (HSE, 2015b).

Occupational health and safety shouldn't be ignored, because research from the United States actually shows that after adjusting for inflation, costs related to accident and injury in the workplace have increased by about US $33 billion annually (OSH, 2012). In a similar vein, rates of stress and related conditions have nearly doubled since the 1970s in the UK (HSE, 2015b). Although fatalities are decreasing in some countries like the UK, it should not be taken for granted that over time, workplaces naturally become safer and better places to work. Psychological, physical and medical health problems can be problematic for employers and employees alike. It should not be assumed that health and safety should be discarded because of a few flippant headlines or the occasional regulation that seems a bit silly. It takes a measured, considered approach to understand what is reasonable and practical.

The business case

The Royal Society for the Prevention of Accidents sets out an excellent business case supporting health and safety in the workplace (RSPA, 2013).

Keeping workplaces safe and healthy looks different in different industries. It may mean construction workers wearing personal protective equipment and being careful not to take unnecessary risks, or rush the work while compromising safety. It might be a restaurant being careful not to serve its customers undercooked chicken, unwashed salads or oysters at the wrong time of year. It's making sure people are properly trained so as not to put themselves or others at unnecessary risk.

Severe accidents, like fires, and severe injuries or deaths at work can be the end of businesses, large and small alike. The more severe the accident, the more difficult it is for the business and the people working within it to recover. Injuries are demotivating and discouraging for others around them – unsafe workplaces are not environments that most people want to work in.

Good systems and processes for making sure the workplace is safe are important, but keep in mind the core focus of health and safety. Particularly for small businesses who may not have the resources, remember health and safety is not just about box checking or paying lip service to the regulations without making any real changes. Health and safety involves two common-sense components:

1 Health and safety is about ensuring the wellbeing of the workforce and the resilience and continuity of the business.
2 Health and safety is an area which requires expertise. More complex workplaces require knowledge and expertise to make them as safe and healthy as possible.

Health and safety is not just another form of political correctness; it's a way of making sure the business is resilient, prepared and runs effectively. Good health and safety practices should be a part of every workplace.

Conclusion

Ignore the silly edicts about blowing bubbles, Santa throwing sweets or banning glasses with handles. In many cases, those are invented by busy bodies but have no real relationship to actual health and safety. Avoid getting distracted by tabloid headlines, and remember workplaces should be as safe and healthy as possible – we don't want them to resemble Victorian workhouses.

References

Bates, C (2009) Time is called on traditional pint glasses after government brands them too dangerous, *Daily Mail*, 24 August. Available at: http://www.dailymail. co.uk/sciencetech/article-1208668/Time-called-traditional-pint-glass-Home-Office-demand-safer-design-reduce-assaults.html

Black, R (2016) Elf and safety gone mad as Northern Ireland councils ban Santa from throwing sweets to children, *Belfast Daily Telegraph*, 9 December. Available at: http://www.belfasttelegraph.co.uk/news/northern-ireland/ elf-and-safety-gone-mad-as-northern-ireland-councils-ban-santa-from-throwing-sweets-to-children-35279780.html

European Agency for Safety and Health at Work (2013) *Estimating the Costs of Accidents and Ill Health at Work: Executive summary*, Publications Office for the European Union, Luxembourg

Health and Safety Executive (HSE) (2015a) *Statistics on Fatal Injuries in the Workplace in Great Britain 2015: Full-year details and technical notes*, Health and Safety Executive

Health and Safety Executive (HSE) (2015b) *Historical Picture: Trends in work-related injuries and ill health in Great Britain since the introduction of the Health and Safety at Work Act 1974*, Health and Safety Executive

Health and Safety Executive (HSE) (2016) *Health and Safety Statistics: Key figures for Great Britain (2015/16)*, Health and Safety Executive

Martin, D (2013) Toothpicks removed from the table, beer glasses with handles scrapped and bubbles banned from child's party: nonsense health and safety edicts that don't actually exist, *Daily Mail*, 2 April. Available at: http://www. dailymail.co.uk/news/article-2303137/Health-safety-nonsense-revealed-Toothpicks-removed-bubbles-banned-childs-party.html

Maclaughlin, S (2016) The end of juicy burgers? Chefs ordered to cook meat patties only 'well done' in food safety crackdown, *Daily Mail*, 28 April. Available at: http://www.dailymail.co.uk/news/article-3564657/Sydney-burger-bars-ordered-cook-meat-patties-health-safety-crackdown.html

Myers, K (2009) Kevin Myers responds to *The Mirror* about 'health and safety gone mad', Health and Safety Executive. Available at: http://www.hse.gov.uk/ press/record/2009/mirror070909.htm

National Safety Council (NSC) (1998) *Accident Facts 1998*, National Safety Council, Itasca, Illinois

Occupational Health and Safety (OSH) (2012) US work-related injuries, illnesses cost $250 billion annually: study, OHS. Available at: https://ohsonline.com/ articles/2012/01/23/us-workrelated-injuries-illnesses-cost-250-billion-annually-study.aspx

Pattinson, R (2016) Door prats: couple's doormat seized after council staff deem it a health and safety risk – and the jobsworths charged them a £40 removal fee, *The Sun*, 2 December. Available at: https://www.thesun.co.uk/news/2309314/

couples-doormat-seized-after-council-staff-deem-it-a-health-and-safety-risk-as-they-are-charged-40-for-removal

Royal Society for the Prevention of Accidents (RSPA) (2013), Making the business case for health and safety, Royal Society for the Prevention of Accidents. Available at: https://www.rospa.com/occupational-safety/advice/business-case

– MYTH 6 –

SURVEILLANCE IMPROVES PERFORMANCE

Surveillance does not just affect those within the organization, because the more surveillance data is collected, the greater the consequences that come with its collection and the more people it can potentially affect.

Introduction

Are workers more or less productive with someone looking over their shoulder? Does surveillance reduce theft and other types of bad behaviour in the workplace? Can monitoring the workplace help to make it safer and more secure?

A large study conducted by Oz, Glass and Behling (1999) examining the effect of surveillance on employee attitudes predictably found that employees believed surveillance would cause increased tensions on the job and have a negative overall impact. A more recent study by Samaranayake and Gamage (2011) showed that the more employees believed their privacy was being violated, the more dissatisfied they were at work.

In his book *1984*, George Orwell imagined a dystopian world of ubiquitous surveillance where:

> It was terribly dangerous to let your thoughts wander when you were in a public place or within range of a telescreen. The smallest thing could give you away. A nervous tic, an unconscious look of anxiety, a habit of muttering to yourself – anything that carried with it the suggestion of abnormality, of having something to hide.

Surveillance is already pervasive in public and private spaces, from CCTV cameras monitoring spaces, to large-scale collection of electronic data, which is only becoming more common in the workplace. If you have a company e-mail account, your employer can access every e-mail you send and receive. If you have an electronic pass to enter different rooms and buildings, your employer can monitor your movements. It is possible for an employer to monitor everything you do on a company computer or mobile phone.

There can be no doubt that surveillance is pervasive, and is somewhere between difficult and impossible to roll back, so the question must be raised: 'How far are we prepared to go?' To explore this, we'll use an example of a company potentially using drones to monitor employee behaviour in work as well as outside of work.

CASE STUDY   An example of extreme surveillance

The example quoted from Orwell may seem fantastical, but in December 2016 the *Guardian* (Opray, 2016) reported that mining giant Rio Tinto was hiring a contractor that would use drones to monitor employees during work as well as during their time off work. They quoted Keith Weston, VP of global sales and business development for the mining giant, as saying that surveillance 'gives us actionable, real-time insights and metrics on equipment and people movement, customer satisfaction, even retail spending. Our goal is to get to the point where we can capture individual insights on where employees are spending their time and money and improve the quality of their lives.'

Later reports (such as Dunstan, 2016) suggested Rio Tinto denied the reports and 'the comments with regards to future technology are conceptual only and there are no intentions to introduce any of these concepts to Rio Tinto sites.' Of course, intentions can always change and the very fact that these types of surveillance may soon be accessible to employers will concern many workers.

While the employers in most cases emphasize that collecting data about their employees can help them to improve performance, identify health or mental health issues and 'capture individual insight' about employees 'and improve the quality of their lives', the psychological effects of pervasive surveillance must also be considered. In their investigation, an unnamed Rio Tinto employee said, 'How focused can you be knowing there's [sic] drones or cameras constantly watching you everywhere you go?' The employee was concerned that constant surveillance would cause more stress and distraction in an already dangerous job.

In relation to this type of surveillance and monitoring that already takes place at the company, a social worker working with these employees said she often hears individuals worrying: 'Does that mean that if I can't sleep well and I decide to go out and look at the stars at midnight that somebody's going to be watching me, and that's going to be "flagged" somewhere and I'm going to be in trouble for it?' That's a remarkably similar concern to that raised in the quote from *1984*.

Excessive surveillance can create suspicion, stress and distrust between employers and employees. It also reduces individual employee autonomy, which is an important part of motivation and improving performance (MacRae and Furnham, 2017). If you take away workers' autonomy and flexibility it dampens their motivation. Pervasive surveillance can send the message that the employer does not trust the employees' ability to do their job independently.

Surveillance and security

Surveillance raises a secondary issue because it involves extensive collection of data and subsequent storage of that data. If companies collect and store detailed data about their employees, their behaviours, conversations, personal strengths and vulnerabilities, how safe is that data?

Let's explore the issue using the recent and controversial Investigatory Powers Act 2016 in the UK. This law requires internet service providers (like Virgin Media, BT, EE, TalkTalk, etc) to record every single website that every single one of their customers has visited for the past year. There are various arguments for and against this type of surveillance that are far beyond the scope of this chapter, but a critical consideration for businesses is not just whether they can afford to store and collect this data, but whether they can afford to *lose* the surveillance data. Consider the case of TalkTalk's catastrophic hack in 2015.

CASE STUDY   Cyber attack at TalkTalk

In October 2015 the telecommunications company TalkTalk was the victim of a cyber attack. Over 150,000 customers had their personal data accessed and over 15,000 customers had their bank details stolen (BBC, 2015). In the aftermath, the company admitted that that single data breach had lost them 95,000 customers and cost them £60 million (Burgess, 2016). A difficult time for the company, but what of the effect on the customers? What of all those with their personal details and, in some cases, private financial information floating around somewhere in the cold vacuum of cyberspace? And what if an entire year of those people's browsing histories had been stolen? Or what if these had been employee records? Or the confidential plans of senior leadership? The implications are extremely concerning.

The hack of TalkTalk should provide a strong note of caution, particularly when considering the criminals who perpetrated the hack. This was not a case of corporate espionage or a political attack from an enemy nation or rogue state. Nor was it a group of activists or ideological group. The ages of those arrested in connection with the crime ranged from 15 to 20. A 17-year-old boy in Norwich pleaded guilty of the hack, saying, 'I didn't think of the consequences at the time. I was just showing off to my mates' (BBC, 2016).

If a large, publicly quoted company with £1.8 billion in annual revenue can lose the data of hundreds of thousands of customers through what appears to have been a group of teenagers fooling around, it must serve as a warning to other companies about what they choose to surveil, along with if, how and where they store that data – and whether they can afford to lose it.

A study commissioned by IBM (Ponemon, 2016) indicated the biggest losses in corporate data breaches were from losing consumer and employee confidence. In their research with 383 companies across 12 countries, they found that data breaches across all the companies cost about US $1.5 billion in total. The more sensitive the data, the more costly and difficult the breach of corporate data was to resolve.

Organizations must have a sober second thought about surveillance. When and if collecting data about employees, such as medical data, details of their movement in their personal and private lives, GPS locations, or other personal and private information, what would be the cost of losing this data or having it stolen?

Surveillance does not just affect those within the organization, because the more surveillance data collected, the greater the consequences that come with its collection and the more people it can potentially affect.

The case of TalkTalk is by no means an exception. For example, in early 2016 the United States Federal Bureau of Investigation and Department of Homeland Security were hacked and tens of thousands of personnel files were compromised; the same hacking group warned they had a vast 200 GB of data from the Department of Justice (McGoogan, 2016). The case of the FBI data breach emphasizes that the consequences of losing basic person-nel files in a security or intelligence organization can be a great concern. If an employee's personal or professional information is hacked or publicly leaked, it can have a devastating effect on employee morale and trust. It can have profoundly damaging effects for company effectiveness, public percep-tions and trust.

And what of the cost of losing sensitive data stored about a leader or leadership team? Hillary Clinton cited the breaches and leaks in her e-mail data as one of the reasons she lost the election for US president (Chuck and Alba, 2016). Whether or not this was an actual reason for her election loss, it highlights how embarrassing and difficult data breaches can be. Leaks and data breaches of personal, sensitive or surveillance information can have lasting and ongoing effects on employees, leaders and entire organizations.

Surveillance and oversight

A final consideration regarding surveillance is whether or not monitoring employees is an effective form of oversight. If you watch people closely enough can you prevent them from stealing? Research from de Vries and Van Gelder (2015) indicated that individual differences in personality are far better predictors of misbehaviour in the workplace (explaining about 34 per cent) than a culture of surveillance (10 per cent). An ethical culture was also more effective at preventing bad behaviour (15 per cent) than surveil-lance. This suggests that surveillance *can* have an effect, but the benefits are relatively minor. The small benefits may not outweigh the consequences.

There are systems and processes that can be put in place to mitigate risks and prevent or mitigate bad behaviour from employees without a pervasive

Table 6.1 Components of surveillance and oversight

	Oversight	Surveillance
Feature	Proactive.	Reactive.
Purpose	To provide a flexible structure that can adapt to different problems if they arise, identify root causes and prevent them when possible.	To identify, record and observe good or bad behaviour when it is displayed.
Structure	Reporting structures, accountabilities and levels of management are in place to identify potential and current problems, and address them from a personal and situational perspective.	Monitoring systems record and store data on employee behaviour to react to events and data.
Responsibilities	Different individuals and groups are accountable for the functioning of the system, all employees are responsible actors in the system.	Technicians and technology are responsible for monitoring and recording data about all individuals, or select groups.
Culture	All individuals are responsible actors within the system, with clearly defined roles and accountabilities.	Employees are conditioned to beware of 'good' behaviours that will be rewarded and 'bad' behaviours that will be punished.
Framework	Flexible structure that is adaptable to change.	Rigid structure with proscribed and prescribed behaviours.

and stifling culture of surveillance. The difference is between *surveillance*, which is a close operation, and *oversight*, which is a less aggressive, more flexible structure for dealing with potential problems (see Table 6.1).

Examples

1 Oversight. The role of oversight in a company is more like watchful, considerate and knowledgeable observation. It may involve being alert to potential warning signs for damage or derailment. It also entails individuals being responsible for acting on and resolving any potential problems

before they become too difficult or too problematic. For example, a board of a large company should ensure the senior leadership is taking appropriate, but not excessive risks and has the right strategic objectives. Yet they are not directly involved in the day-to-day operations nor do they issue diktats – they observe and guide instead of surveilling and controlling.

2 **Surveillance.** An example of a surveillance system is when a company collects and stores copies of all employee e-mails. This may not have any stated purpose other than monitoring, collecting and storing all employee communication. It may or may not be used, read or analysed by others within the organization.

Conclusion

Surveillance is not necessarily an effective method to improve productivity. That is not to say that surveillance shouldn't be used, but it is a reminder that any data that is collected from or about employees needs to be carefully considered. What are the benefits of collecting that information and what could go wrong?

Surveillance can reduce autonomy and increase suspicion and distress amongst employees. Collecting and storing sensitive surveillance data can create a great deal of corporate risk. Surveillance can have very limited effects in reducing bad behaviour, but does little to promote creativity, independence, autonomous motivation or to improve overall performance. All individuals and companies need to be extremely cautious about collecting and protecting surveillance information. Assume there is a strong possibility that surveillance information could be stolen or leaked eventually: is the benefit worth the price?

References

BBC (2015) TalkTalk hack 'affected 157,000 customers', BBC, 6 November. Available at: http://www.bbc.com/news/business-34743185

BBC (2016) Boy, 17, admits to TalkTalk hacking offences, BBC, 15 November. Available at: http://www.bbc.com/news/uk-37990246

Burgess, M (2016) TalkTalk hack toll: 100k customers and £60m, *Wired*, 2 February. Available at: http://www.wired.co.uk/article/talktalk-hack-customers-lost

Chuck, E and Alba, M (2016) Hillary Clinton partially blames loss on FBI Director James Comey's email inquiry, CNBC, 12 November. Available at: http://www.nbcnews.com/politics/2016-election/hillary-clinton-partially-blames-loss-fbi-director-james-comeys-email-n683046

de Vries, R E and Van Gelder, J (2015) Explaining workplace delinquency: the role of honest-humility, ethical culture, and employee surveillance, *Personality and Individual Differences*, 86, pp 112–16

Dunstan, J (2016) Rio Tinto rules out drone surveillance of workers on Pilbara FIFO camps, Australian Broadcasting Corporation, 8 December. Available at: http://www.abc.net.au/news/2016-12-09/rio-tinto-rules-out-drone-surveillance-of-workers/8107758

MacRae, I and Furnham, A (2017) *Motivation and Performance: A guide to managing a diverse workforce*, Kogan Page, London

McGoogan, C (2016) Thousands of FBI and Homeland Security details stolen by hackers, *Telegraph*, 8 February. Available at: http://www.telegraph.co.uk/technology/2016/02/08/thousands-of-fbi-and-homeland-security-details-stolen-by-hackers

Opray, M (2016) Revealed: Rio Tinto's plan to use drones to monitor workers' private lives, *Guardian*, 7 December. Available at: https://www.theguardian.com/world/2016/dec/08/revealedrio-tinto-surveillance-station-plans-to-use-drones-to-monitors-staffs-private-lives

Orwell, G (1949/2004) *Nineteen Eighty-Four (1984)* Penguin Classics, Penguin, Harmondsworth

Oz, E, Glass, R and Behling, R (1999) Electronic workplace monitoring: what employees think, *International Journal of Management Science*, 27, pp 167–77

Ponemon Institute (2016) 2016 Cost of data breach study: global analysis, IBM. Available at: https://securityintelligence.com/media/2016-cost-data-breach-study/

Samaranayake, V and Gamage, C (2011) Employee perception towards electronic monitoring at work place and its impact on job satisfaction of software professionals in Sri Lanka, *Telematics and Informatics*, 29, pp 233–44

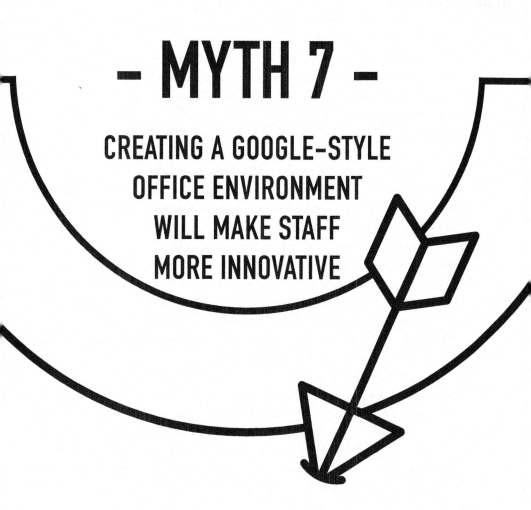

– MYTH 7 –

CREATING A GOOGLE-STYLE OFFICE ENVIRONMENT WILL MAKE STAFF MORE INNOVATIVE

Companies will always benefit from offering perks and rewards to their employees when their employees value the perks on offer.

Introduction

Technology companies and start-ups like Google have changed workplace culture in a number of ways, trying to make the office environment fun, quirky, unique and in some cases infantile. They have been consistent in creating certain types of office culture, starting with strange interview questions and changing the nature of the office environment. But is this change for better or for worse? And are there more factors behind these trends than just making work 'fun'?

Rachel Feintzeig (2015), in an article for the *Wall Street Journal*, describes what changes Google has made to its office environment, and how these changes are starting to become more mainstream. While boring, sterile office environments seem to be the norm, Silicon Valley companies like Google are trying to compete for top talent by making the office environment more fun and engaging. They bring entertainments like full-sized basketball courts, golf simulation video games and big-screen TVs. They may offer company-funded meals with the latest food trends, or fully stocked fridges. They also may have slightly more infantile perks on-site, like ball pits or playgrounds. Is this all just a bit of fun and games, or does it actually make for a better working environment and better workers?

An interesting criticism of Google-style, open office plans in trendy warehouses is nicely direct. Open-plan offices are cheaper because they use less space, are less expensive to build and are a trend that is spreading rapidly (Kaufman, 2014). But the drawbacks of open-plan and shared office space are obvious – people get more distracted, end up chatting more and working less, cannot have privacy and end up reporting lower rates of satisfaction and productivity (Kim and de Dear, 2013).

An article in the *New Yorker* provides an interesting analysis of how open-plan offices make people feel better and closer to their colleagues, but those benefits just mask a decline in performance that results from being less focused and productive (Konnikova, 2014). In a review of the research on open office plans, Hodgkinson et al (2011) found that they reduce productivity, attention spans and creative thinking. The reality is that being surrounded by noise and distractions is not good for overall productivity.

On ball pits and espresso machines

Is it condescending?

Another factor to consider is the office environment, and whether the office culture fits the atmosphere. We spoke to a few central London office workers at multinational companies. While some people may like ping pong tables and ball pits, many people find that type of culture and those benefits to be condescending. Making work more enjoyable, healthy and engaging is one thing, but it can seem strange to many people that for some employers the way to attract young talent is to infantilize and condescend to them.

There are genuine benefits that some employers offer that contribute to actual wellbeing, like on-site physicians, mental health support, access to health and fitness facilities, cafeterias with good food, maternity benefits and flexitime. Is having a playground in that open-plan office really better than other benefits that have real physical and mental health advantages, or that increase wellbeing and productivity?

The more cynical (anonymous) workers we interviewed suspected these more infantile benefits were a ploy to keep people on-site, in the office, and working longer.

Is it a cynical move to keep people in the office longer?

If perks like those described by Stewart (2013) – gourmet office cafeterias, on-site video games and 'fun' activities – are available in the workplace, why would the workers ever leave? Some more cynical critics would say that even if it reduces productivity, it keeps workers on-site. If you have everything you want or need in the office and are rewarded for staying longer hours, why would you leave?

On silly interview questions

There is a trend in creative and technology companies for using excessive creativity in the selection process. Sometimes, relevant, focused and important questions are exchanged for silly questions that are designed to assess how people react in unexpected or unprepared situations. Some creative and emerging companies seem to delight in outdoing each other with silly interview questions. Unfortunately, these silly interview questions often become fatuous and irrelevant when they stray so far from the realm of the actual skills and abilities relevant to the work. Some would argue that strange or unconventional questions test creativity. The problem is, they lead people toward conversations that would be more appropriate at the Mad Hatter's tea party than at a professional job interview for a start-up or multinational company.

Silly interview questions fall in line with some of the more unconventional design elements of the Google-style office environment. They are meant to be frivolous (perhaps innovative, or at least different) but may not overtly have a purpose. They both deserve the same criticism though: is this just a bit of fun, or does it have a specific point? To justify the frivolous environment or interview question, there should be evidence that it has some benefit.

Standard interview questions about where you studied, what you've learned most from previous experience, what you want to get from the job and what you can offer may seem a bit dull. So what about the alternatives? The examples below may seem ridiculous, but they are documented interview questions.

- If you were a jelly bean, what colour would you be?
- What does creativity smell like?

Google is one company that popularized these type of interview questions, using questions like 'How many petrol stations are there in the US?', 'How many golf balls can you fit into a classic American school bus?' and 'Why are manhole covers round?' (Doré, 2014).

Asking people out-of-the-box questions tests only one thing: how people react to those or similar out-of-the-box questions. They purportedly measure the candidate's ability to be innovative or solve an unexpected problem. Yet the problem is, there are better, more useful and more relevant questions that will better predict performance if they are more related to the job. These types of off-the-wall questions may be useful in a call centre or for a technical support hotline, but there is little you will learn about how someone will do their job if the questions are unrelated to the job. If you ask someone, 'If you were lost in the Sahara Desert with only a silver letter opener, four dozen lemons and bottle of gin, would you rather have a camel or a peregrine falcon?', their answer will probably not be very relevant to an everyday work situation.

Employers, particularly those in the technology sector, always seem to be finding new ways to assess creativity and embarrass interviewees. Silly questions are extremely unlikely to help an interviewer understand whether a candidate has the proper qualifications or knowledge, whether they can navigate a Word document, contribute to the morning meeting or appropriately handle customer service or client relations.

Eccentric interview questions likely reveal more about the personality deficits of the interviewer than anything relevant about the interviewee's answers.

Ditch the strange and eccentric interview questions and keep these three rules in mind:

1 Keep questions and interview framework consistent. The interview questions should be closely aligned with core competencies and the demands of the job. Unless the person's job is going to be filling school buses with golf balls, that's not a relevant or a useful question to ask. Ask questions that are specifically targeted to the skills, knowledge or behaviour needed to do the job.

2 Make sure all interviewers are working from the same framework, and that they are all briefed in the same way. This is closely related to the first point, because if multiple people are interviewing job candidates, they should be evaluating and scoring in the same way. Interviewers can have their own (occasionally bizarre) ideas about what a successful candidate looks like. Some people don't like redheads, some people prefer people of certain genders or ethnicities. Some people get on well with someone who likes the same sports team or political party – all irrelevant to actual job performance. If there are multiple interviewers, each interviewer should be making similar judgements based on a common set of criteria.

3 Focus on desirable *and* undesirable criteria. Find and identify the factors to 'select in' as well as 'select out'. Sometimes people who seem creative, engaging or interview well are not the best candidates but can hide their derailment potential behind charm or bluff. Be aware of dark-side and possible derailing traits such as narcissism and manipulativeness. Have a check list for 'bad' behaviours as well as 'good' attributes. Does the candidate dodge questions, talk over the interviewer and boast about their achievements? Do their references and history corroborate what they say in an interview? Do these behaviours check the 'yes' or the 'no' box?

Culture should fit benefits

It is important to compare and contrast organizational culture with the benefits and perks the company offers. Company scooters and playgrounds may seem superficial and trite in organizations where those perks do not match the culture. A person might be extremely concerned if their accountant liked to spend their lunch hour in a children's playground or if their lawyer charged their fees in Haribos.

There may be a case to be made for innovative or creative companies in the technology or creative sphere to offer perks and benefits that may seem to be out of place or silly in a conventional office. There is a good case to be made for companies like adventure travel company G Adventures to offer employees fantastic perks and bonuses in travel (MacRae and Furnham, 2017).

Companies will always benefit from offering perks and rewards to their employees when their employees value the perks on offer. All elements of the HR process, from selection and promotion interviews to policies, rewards and bonuses will benefit from aligning with office culture. But it is important to be wary of HR and business trends that have little evidence of being effective. Sometimes successful companies do silly things, and some companies with a great deal of revenue find interesting and creative ways of wasting their money. It is best to look for the evidence behind why (and if!) a policy is successful, before jumping on the bandwagon of a new workplace fad.

Conclusion

Workplaces, workplace culture and HR practices are improving. Work is getting better for many people and helping workers to be happier, more engaged and more productive in their work, but every new idea is not necessarily a good one. Imitating certain practices of successful companies is not a surefire way to success. If fun, novel or interesting business practices work for a certain company, they will not necessarily work for everyone. Evaluate HR practices critically, and use evidence (not anecdote) to choose the best.

References and further reading

Doré, L (2014) The 11 hardest Google interview questions, *Indy100*. Available at: https://www.indy100.com/article/the-11-hardest-google-job-interview-questions--bJ3gJX2wQe

Feintzeig, R (2015) Google-style office perks go mainstream, *Wall Street Journal*, 4 August. Available at: https://www.wsj.com/articles/google-style-office-perks-go-mainstream-1438680780

Furnham, A, Tsivrikos, D and MacRae, I (2018) *The Psychology of Behaviour at Work: The individual in the organization*, 3rd edn, Psychology Press, London

Hodgkinson, G P et al (2011) The physical environment of the office: contemporary and emerging issues, *Industrial Review of Industrial and Organizational Psychology*, 26, pp 193–235

Kaufman, L (2014) Google got it wrong: the open-plan office trend is destroying the workplace, *Washington Post*, 30 December. Available at: https://www.washingtonpost.com/posteverything/wp/2014/12/30/google-got-it-wrong-the-open-office-trend-is-destroying-the-workplace/

Kim, J and de Dear, R (2013) Workplace satisfaction: the privacy-communication trade-off in open-plan offices, *Journal of Environmental Psychology*, **36**, pp 18–26

Konnikova, M (2014) The open-office trap, *New Yorker*, 7 January. Available at: http://www.newyorker.com/business/currency/the-open-office-trap

MacRae, I and Furnham, A (2017) *Motivation and Performance: A guide to motivating a diverse workforce*, Kogan Page, London

Stewart, J B (2013) Looking for a lesson in Google's perks, *New York Times*. Available at: http://www.nytimes.com/2013/03/16/business/at-google-a-place-to-work-and-play.html

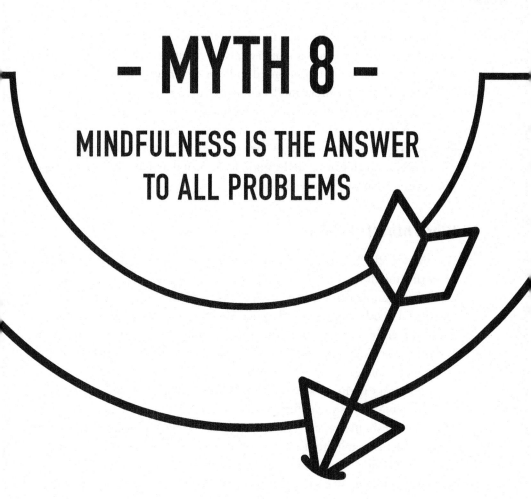

– MYTH 8 –

MINDFULNESS IS THE ANSWER TO ALL PROBLEMS

*Mindfulness is not just a namby-pamby new-age gimmick,
but it is far from being a magic bullet.*

Introduction

What mindfulness is not

Instead of starting with a description of what we mean by mindfulness, this chapter would be better served by starting with what mindfulness *is not*. Let's dispel the first part of any myths and preconceptions about mindfulness right from the beginning, then ease into a more clear and useful look at the topic.

Mindfulness does not require any spiritual, new-age mysticism or pseudo-science. Mindfulness is not about crystals or chanting, it has nothing to do with juice cleanses, and doesn't need to be done while sitting on bean bags or holding hands in a circle and listening to Enya.

All of those activities may use or combine the concept of mindfulness for their own purposes. They may use mindfulness effectively in combination with other rituals or activities (or they may not). But mindfulness is a separate concept which can be understood as a mental activity apart from any spirituality, religiosity or pseudoscience.

What mindfulness is

Konnikova (2012) presents an interesting and helpful personification of practising mindfulness, distinct from Buddhist monks or yoga retreats, using a familiar example from English literature. The example is of a rigorous, thoughtful sleuth who is both analytical and meditative. He quiets his mind, focuses intently on the world around him, and is keenly aware of current reality surrounding him and his own thought processes. This literary figure is Sherlock Holmes.

Mindfulness is the process of quietly and personally detaching oneself and observing one's surroundings and emotions as a dispassionate observer. Instead of instantly reacting to emotions, thoughts or compulsions, the person practising mindfulness watches the thoughts as they come and go, ebbing and fading. Instead of *rumination*, which is the excessive focus on particular thoughts that latches onto stress and amplifies anxiety, mindfulness involves acknowledging the thought as if observing it in someone else, without dwelling on it. Indeed, the scientific research shows that rumination increases stress and anxiety (Querstret and Cropley, 2013) while mindfulness can reduce stress (Rosenzweig et al, 2010; Carlson et al, 2003).

When it works

One of the most tangible benefits of mindfulness is that it can reduce stress at work. In a meta analysis of 39 mindfulness studies, Hoffman and colleagues (2010) found that mindfulness helped to reduce stress and improve psychological wellbeing. This is because mindfulness training can help people process emotions differently and more effectively.

Another way in which mindfulness can be a strong asset in the workplace is that it can improve focus. It helps people to ignore unnecessary distractions. This means employees who practise mindfulness improve their focus on tasks and consequently perform better at work compared with those who do not practise mindfulness training (Ortner, Kilner and Zelazo, 2007).

There is a great deal of research which indicates mindfulness training can improve creativity (or cognitive flexibility, as the researchers refer to it). The mindfulness training helps to develop mental flexibility, disengages rigid thinking and consequently allows workers to be open to new information or novel solutions to problems (Davis and Hayes, 2012).

The reduction in stress and increased emotional control that results from mindfulness training can have a host of first- and second-order benefits. The reduction in stress from mindfulness training has also been implicated in improving quality of sleep, decreasing blood pressure, improving energy levels and boosting the immune system. Improving employee wellbeing can greatly improve worker performance and productivity (MacRae and Furnham, 2017).

When it might not work

The research on mindfulness shows that it is a promising technique to reduce stress, increase focus and mitigate distracting or counterproductive behaviours. But it is necessary to be aware that, though it can have benefits from the medical to the professional, it should be seen as a useful addition but not as a substitute. For example, even though mindfulness has been found to reduce pain amongst patients with chronic pain (eg Rosenzweig et al, 2010), the conclusion was that it was useful as *complementary* to the medical treatment but not as a replacement.

There are other criticisms concerning mindfulness. Much of the research findings which indicate positive effects of mindfulness use well-planned and implemented mindfulness training projects (Baer, 2003). However, like any course of treatment, mindfulness has to be done well to have positive effects. It is unlikely that reading a short article in a popular magazine then trying to meditate for a few minutes is going to have much of an effect. To be effective, mindfulness needs to be learned and developed, often with the help of an instructor or teacher.

Others have criticized mindfulness because it can have potentially unexpected, even troubling effects (Foster, 2016). One should not necessarily assume that delving deeply into one's own thoughts and emotions is always an easy or enjoyable experience. Sometimes heightening one's awareness of one's own thoughts, emotions and experiences can bring troubling or concerning thoughts or emotions to the forefront of one's mind. For example, when someone is experiencing a great deal of stress (and when mindfulness is not properly practised, or is practised without sufficient guidance), being mindful of that stress can amplify it. Like psychological or medical guidance, mindfulness should be practised and cultivated with a qualified and knowledgeable practitioner, advisor or expert.

If someone is undergoing medical treatment because they have cancer, mindfulness might help to reduce the pain or anxiety they are experiencing but does nothing to treat the underlying condition or the effects of the cancer. Mindfulness is not a replacement for proper medical treatment or good HR practice; it is an additional tool that can be useful and complement other methods. This is equally applicable to the workplace. If someone is being bullied or harassed in the workplace, mindfulness training and practice might help to mitigate some of the stress that person experiences and help them to identify the source of their stress, but it does not resolve the real issue.

Conclusion

Mindfulness is a well-demonstrated tool that can help to reduce stress, mitigate anxiety, and improve focus and productivity. Mindfulness is not just a namby-pamby new-age gimmick. It is useful and effective, but at the same time it is far from being a magic bullet. Mindfulness is not a replacement for good HR practice, but should be seriously considered as another tool in the toolbox for increasing productivity and resilience.

Also, it is important to remember that mindfulness is not automatically or necessarily useful for everyone. It may not help everyone and for some it can reveal troubling or difficult thoughts or emotions. Like any effective workplace intervention, mindfulness should be developed with proper guidance and support.

References

Baer, R A (2003) Mindfulness training as a clinical intervention: a conceptual and empirical review, *Clinical Psychology: Science and practice*, 10 (2), pp 125–43

Carlson, L E et al (2003) Mindfulness-based stress reduction in relation to quality of life, mood, symptoms of stress, and immune parameters in breast and prostate cancer outpatients, *Psychosomatic Medicine*, 65 (4), pp 571–81

Davis, D M and Hayes, J A (2012) What are the benefits of mindfulness? *Monitor on Psychology*, **43** (7), p 64

Foster, D (2016) Is mindfulness making us ill? *Guardian*, 23 January. Available at: https://www.theguardian.com/lifeandstyle/2016/jan/23/is-mindfulness-making-us-ill

Hoffman, S G et al (2010) The effect of mindfulness-based therapy on anxiety and depression: a meta-analytic review, *Journal of Consulting and Clinical Psychology*, **78** (2), pp 169–83

Konnikova, M (2012) The power of concentration, *New York Times*, 15 December. Available at: http://www.nytimes.com/2012/12/16/opinion/sunday/the-power-of-concentration.html

MacRae, I and Furnham, A (2017) *Motivation and Performance: A guide to motivating a diverse workforce*, Kogan Page, London

Ortner, C N M, Kilner, S J and Zelazo, P D (2007) Mindfulness, meditation and reduced emotional interference on a cognitive task, *Motivation and Emotion*, **31**, pp 271–83

Querstret, D and Cropley, M (2013) Assessing treatments used to reduce rumination and/or worry: a systematic review, *Clinical Psychology Review*, **33** (8), pp 996–1009

Rosenzweig, S et al (2010) Mindfulness-based stress reduction for chronic pain conditions: variation in treatment outcomes and role of home meditation practice, *Journal of Psychosomatic Research*, **68**, pp 29–36

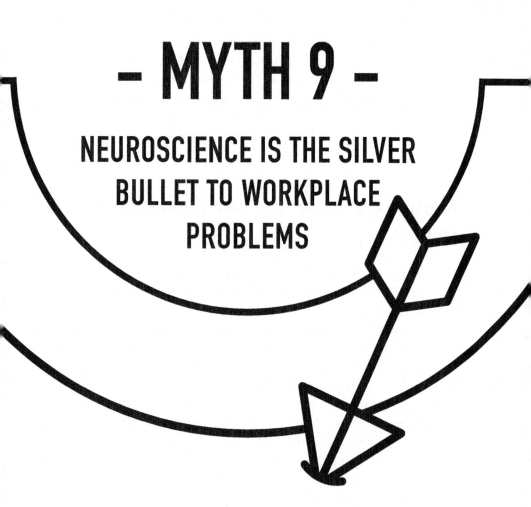

- MYTH 9 -

NEUROSCIENCE IS THE SILVER BULLET TO WORKPLACE PROBLEMS

*Be cautious about separating basic scientific ideas
with unfounded, unverified or silly claims.*

Introduction

Neuroscience is the study of the brain and the body's entire nervous system, but the term is often used to describe the study of the mind and brain in particular. All of the body's processes, thoughts, emotions and all of the ways people behave are controlled within the brain. The study of neuroscience has blossomed through the later part of the 20th century and continues to progress rapidly.

Although this is a rapidly developing field of research, there is still a great deal that is not known about the capability and workings of the human brain (Bear, Connors and Paradiso, 2015). There are some less-than-scrupulous and less-than-knowledgeable people who use it to sell products without using the evidence that is readily available and developing. So is neuroscience really worth the hype, and can it unlock solutions to workplace problems?

Cautionary study: the tale of the dead salmon

Bennett and colleagues (2009) conducted research and subsequently published a brilliantly wry scientific paper using an fMRI to measure the 'neural' activity of a salmon.

The researchers put a dead Atlantic salmon (18 inches long, weighing 3.8 lb) into an fMRI scanner, attempting to measure the blood flow in the salmon's brain while they administered an 'open-ended mentalizing task'. This involved showing a series of photographs of human faces to the salmon and asking it to think about what emotions each of the people pictured was feeling. The researchers used various calibrations for the brain-scanning equipment and found that two small areas of the salmon's brain 'responded to the task'. An unsophisticated or humourless reader of the paper might conclude that the researchers had found the part of a dead salmon's brain that responds to human emotions.

The other explanation was clearly explained by the researchers: 'Could we conclude from this data that the salmon is engaging in perspective taking [understanding others' emotions]? Certainly not.' They concluded that their findings highlighted a limit in specific measures of brain activity and went on to explain their results as just noise, random effects unrelated to the salmon's 'task'. The researchers (Bennett et al, 2009) recommend being more careful with research methods and caution researchers about using overly simplistic explanations. Using the tools improperly or in an uninformed way can create random variations or wildly inaccurate results.

This study should not be interpreted to mean that neuroscience is not a valid science, nor should it be used to say that imaging methods which measure activity in the brain do not work. The key message is that one needs to be wary of neuroscience research that is not done well, or is used to support conclusions that do not hold water.

Cautionary example 1: the Royal Bank of Scotland can't actually read your mind

A 2017 story in the *Huffington Post* (Gray, 2017) extraordinarily and dubiously claimed: 'Deciding what kind of job you want after university can be daunting.' But goes on to say they have a solution! 'The Royal Bank of Scotland has developed an ingenious solution to this problem – by "reading" students' minds.' Before even starting to debunk this claim, it could be useful to note that the Royal Bank of Scotland (RBS) would have performed much differently over the past decade if they were really able to read minds.

RBS hires a company which uses an EEG cap with electrodes that measure electrical activity on the surface of the brain. Then, participants are shown a series of 10 images and videos which apparently are linked to a specific skill or ability. Based on the electrical activity in the brain, the machine then apparently identifies courses the participant might find most interesting (which it certainly cannot). Matt Wall, neuroscientist at Hammersmith Hospital, explains that this is not the right kind of neuroimaging machine to even approach this kind of work; it would take dozens of hours instead of a few minutes to do anything close to what they claim and even then it has a great deal of limitations. He says, 'The idea that you can just stick this headset on someone and read it off is ridiculous' (Chivers, 2017).

Even if this is (and it is) complete neurobabble, the article seemingly unintentionally identifies the real reason RBS find this approach useful. Their head of marketing says that 'Our campus tour has been central to our candidate attraction campaign this year – it grabs attention on busy campuses and allows us to have valuable conversations with students who perhaps wouldn't have normally considered financial services for an internship or graduate programme.' Even if it's useless, it gets RBS noticed in a crowded room, and gives them a sort of credibility that their share performance may not.

Cautionary example 2: does your mind look the same piloting a jet plane as it does driving a Porsche?

An even more ridiculous example comes from a 2015 advertising campaign by the luxury car makers Porsche. The slick marketing video seemed to make the claim that piloting a jet fighter had the same effect on an actor's brain as driving quickly in a Porsche.

We will only touch on this example briefly because it takes neurobabble to such an unbelievable level of inaccuracy that is not worth spending very much time on. The actor begins by flying a jet plane, supposedly while hooked up to an EEG head cap. His head bobs and thrashes around like a balloon in a tumble dryer while a 'scientist' supposedly explains the effect this is having on the actor's brain. The biggest problem here is that this type of measurement needs the participant to keep their head absolutely still. Even a twitch of an eyebrow or a smile can completely ruin the measurement. What this video shows is about as accurate as putting a thermometer in a microwave to measure the temperature outdoors (note: please do not try that at home).

It would be easy to spend dozens of pages explaining the specific details of what was wrong with the Porsche advert and why it is scientifically ridiculous, but instead let us move swiftly along in the knowledge that its attempt at 'neuromarketing' falls firmly and completely within the realm of neurobabble.

What to look for

Many articles start by accurately describing a concept (like neuroscience, intelligence, etc) then deftly move from fairly accurate descriptions of the science into wild claims supported only by some fringe practitioner's views or random and often unrelated anecdotes. For example, an article might start by describing what neuroscience is and some of the tools scientists use to measure activity in the brain, like an MRI machine which measures blood flow to identify which regions of the brain are most active during the time of measurement. Then the article might seamlessly (but more often jarringly) lurch into sillier territory.

The sillier neurobabble articles may go on to describe how:

We spoke to a man holding a cardboard sign, raving at passersby outside University College London to understand some of the more practical implications of this neuroscience research. 'I think the government will probably use this for mind control – in fact, they already are and I can prove it telepathically', says the man we will call David (53, unemployed). We then spoke to a famous guru (an entirely invented, serial offender in the realm of neurobabble) who explained, 'I think this recent research proves all of my previous beliefs about the power of the mind over matter... even though I don't really understand the science.'

Often these types of articles introduce some vaguely credible facts before swiftly moving into realms of fantastical clickbait or sensational marketing claims.

Be cautious about combining basic scientific ideas with unfounded, unverified or silly claims.

Conclusion

Neuroscience is an incredibly powerful science that is developing rapidly. There is promising and useful neuroscience research, but the field is still relatively new and developing. At the same time, the word 'neuro' is often used to market the same old snake oil with a different label.

References

Bear, M F, Connors, B and Paradiso, M (2015) Neuroscience: Exploring the brain, Lippincott, Williams and Wilkins, Philadelphia

Bennett, C M et al (2009) Neural correlates of interspecies perspectives taking in the post-mortem Atlantic Salmon: an argument for multiple comparisons correction, NeuroImage, 47 (1)

Chivers, T (2017) No, RBS can't read your mind and tell you if you ought to work in banking, BuzzFeed News, 4 January. Available at: https://www.buzzfeed.com/tomchivers/the-magic-hat-said-rbs-but-i-was-really-hoping-for-slytherin?utm_term=.djV3xyoVzy#.bhpJYvWrVv

Gray, J (2017) Royal Bank of Scotland uses brain scanning technology to help fill top graduate positions. Huffington Post, 3 January. Available at: http://www.huffingtonpost.co.uk/entry/royal-bank-of-scotland-uses-brain-scanning-technology-to-help-fill-top-graduate-positions_uk_586b8503e4b0f24da6e966f0

Porsche (2015) A corkscrew vs a left turn. Porsche. Uncommon. YouTube, 21 April. Available at: https://www.youtube.com/watch?v=o1huW9RMgkM

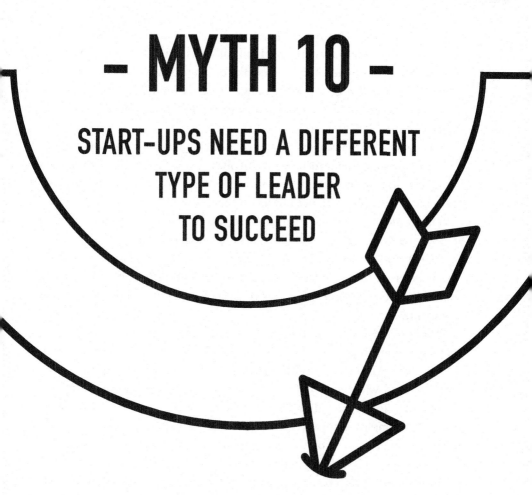

– MYTH 10 –

START-UPS NEED A DIFFERENT TYPE OF LEADER TO SUCCEED

Companies, industries, sectors and the economy may change, but the traits of a good leader remain consistent.

Introduction

A strong leader with a clear vision and the capability to implement it is important to any company, and is especially important for new businesses and start-ups. But too often an aggressive and macho leadership style is mistaken for strength. An informal, shoot-from-the-hip culture may seem edgy and innovative when it is really just disorganized.

Some people imagine that to be innovative or 'disruptive', new companies and start-ups need a different type of person to take control. Jeffrey Hull

(2016), writing in the *Harvard Business Review*, describes this misconception about leadership in start-ups. Hull calls this a 'visionary entrepreneur' type of leadership where the leaders take on a university student approach, working late nights, getting things done at the last minute. They provide a broad vision and model a strong work ethic, developing personal connections within a close-knit group.

Of course, entrepreneurs do have different traits than senior leaders. Entrepreneurs tend to be more involved with the details of their own company and business while senior leaders tend to be more strategic and delegate the details. Both need to have a big vision.

One could argue that being aggressive, disorganized, informal and vulgar doesn't matter as long as they are leading their company to success. But as Dan Lyons writes in the *New York Times* (2017) about many leaders in the start-up tech industry: 'The real problem with tech bros is not just that they're boorish... It's that they're boorish and don't know how to run companies.'

The problem is, this approach to leadership may (or may not) be helpful for small companies or start-ups in the early stages of the business. As businesses grow, it is impossible for the leader to maintain that culture, the close relationships with every employee and the fly-by-the-seat-of-your-pants approach to leadership. Hull (2016) explains that many small start-ups have 0 per cent employee turnover in their early years, but as they expand the turnover often rockets to 40 per cent by their third year.

As the business scales up, increases revenue, has a larger turnover, more employees and an increasingly segmented workforce, the leadership style needs to evolve or adapt to the business growth. Sometimes a small, close-knit team with friendly and informal relationships can work for a small, niche start-up. However, it can and does lead to toxic and destructive cultures, as we will explore by looking at the recent emergence of 'bro culture'.

'Bro culture'

It's often referred to as 'bro culture' – a problem that has been an issue in the workplace, particularly in start-ups and the tech industry increasingly over recent years (Minter, 2017). Somehow, younger entrepreneurs have managed to revive what used to be referred to as the 'old boys' club' and combine it with frat-house culture. It refers to a culture that is aggressive and impulsive, full of bravado but typically with an ambivalent relationship with the truth. It's about inflated stock prices and aggressive business decisions based more on personality and showing off than sensible or responsible decision making.

The leaders in this culture tend to be characterized by immature and reckless decision making. Businesses are run with a focus on short-term profit and aggressive growth, irrespective of the long-term consequences and also without attention to regulations, good business practice or the effect it has on other employees (especially those outside the 'bro' group).

The other feature of bro culture is that it tends to be misogynistic and discriminate openly or implicitly against anyone who doesn't fit the model of free-wheeling, chest-thumping, bellicose masculinity. Lyons (2017) describes it as a culture where 'women get hired, but they rarely get promoted and sometimes complain of being harassed. Minorities and older workers are excluded.'

The culture of the company and acceptable behaviour comes from the leadership at the top (MacRae and Furnham, 2014). When the leadership has an attitude that their company should be run for their own entertainment, that attitude filters down and across the company and is contagious. These companies tend to have serious problems with unethical behaviour, including a preponderance of misogyny, groping and sexual harassment complaints (Illing, 2017).

'Bro culture' in the military

In the next section, we will discuss bro culture in the tech industry, because there has been recent attention on the problems with it in Silicon Valley and tech start-ups. Before this toxic type of culture was highly criticized in Silicon Valley, it was identified in the US military. Looking at the effects of bro culture in the military highlights the problems often associated with it, and how severe and destructive the consequences can be.

The problem of a hyper-masculine yet immature corporate culture is nothing new, but bro culture has also been criticized in the US military (Sorcher, 2013). It's a unique workplace, but also a workplace culture where sexual assault and harassment is rampant. Some criticize the hyper-masculine environment of the US armed forces, old traditions from an organization that used to be all male, or the challenges of the demands of the job.

Yet it's not a question of what level of assault or harassment between colleagues is acceptable, and for the US armed forces it is even more straightforward than in private-sector companies where office romances may be consensual and appropriate. In the military, like all other aspects of the work, there are specific rules and regulations for sexual conduct. It's supposed to be completely unacceptable – for soldiers, sex is a no-go area. All military bases are supposed to be sex-free zones. Officers cannot date their subordinates. The US military has tried to forbid any sexual contact, but it hasn't worked.

It's one example of a 'bro' culture where an in-group protect each other and collude in unethical behaviour. Any organization or company that develops or promotes this type of culture is in for short- and long-term problems.

The example of the tech industry

There are a multitude of examples of toxic 'bro culture' from the tech industry in Silicon Valley. It's an industry with inflated valuations, braggadocious marketing strategies and massive amounts of investment money poured into projects, many of which never materialize. That's not to say this is true of all tech start-ups, but it is an industry that has an astounding amount of money poured into vague and often fruitless ideas.

Take the example of Quirky, a 'social product development platform'. It was founded in 2009 by Ben Kaufman, who raised US $185 million, but the company managed to get through those millions in relatively short order and went bankrupt because of fundamental problems with the business and mistakes by leadership (Lyons, 2017).

Uber has also been reported to exhibit problems with its leadership culture. Recent reports of sexual harassment within Uber by publications like the *New York Times* (Lyons, 2017) and *Vox* (Illing, 2017) highlight the problem. A former Uber employee, engineer Susan Fowler, wrote that she was sexually harassed and management ignored her claims, saying that the person accused of harassment was a high performer so they 'didn't feel comfortable punishing him. And later that after repeated harassment complaints, Fowler was essentially told that her complaints were the problem, not the behaviour she was complaining about.'

The problem of harassment goes beyond just the victim (although that impact should not be minimized). A culture of discrimination, harassment, impulsive decision making and bravado over substance and sound business decisions is toxic. Certain industries have managed to reinvigorate tired, old and fundamentally counterproductive cultures where the company is run for the enjoyment of senior leadership and their inner circle.

The bottom line is that this type of culture and management style is not good for productivity, profit or the bottom line.

What to do about it?

The *Guardian*, with PricewaterhouseCoopers (Minter, 2017) offers a few tips for digital start-ups to deal with bro culture. The recommendations can be generalized to any start-up and, indeed, any company:

1 **Ask honest for honest feedback.** Be open to hearing both positive and negative feedback, and don't argue with what they say. Ask for honest feedback and be receptive to it.

2 **Institute a zero-tolerance policy for harassment.** Harassment and sexual harassment have no place in the workplace. Make sure there is a formal zero-tolerance policy for sexual harassment and that it is enforced in practice.

3 **Ask former employees.** Check with former employees to understand why they left and what the company was like when they worked there. Ask for honest opinions and be receptive to what former employees say. If necessary, pay them for their time and honesty.

4 **Hire a proper HR expert or team.** Start-ups and small companies often skimp on HR. Entrepreneurs, leaders and others within a small company may be good people, but are no substitute for HR professionals in a growing business.

5 **Grow with the business.** Businesses grow as they change, as should leaders in the company. The best people who start a company are unlikely to be able to fill all the necessary roles as they expand, so they need to grow within the business and hire people to fill the needs of an expanding company.

What makes a good leader?

Companies, industries, sectors and the economy may change, but the traits of a good leader remain consistent. Along with intelligence, knowledge, motivation and ability there are six fundamental traits that good leaders exhibit (MacRae and Furnham 2014).

1 **Conscientiousness.** Conscientiousness is someone's motivation and drive to achieve constructive long-term goals. High conscientiousness means strong planning, goal-directed behaviour and discipline. Strategic thinking is impossible without high conscientiousness. Low-conscientiousness leaders are those whose organizations will be governed entirely by strategy. They may be brilliant at negotiating last-minute situations, adapting to opportunities, and being decisive even when they do not know what is going on. Those with higher conscientiousness tend to be more internally motivated, while those with lower conscientiousness are motivated externally, by people or circumstances around them.

2 **Adjustment.** Adjustment is how someone reacts to stress. Being able to cope with high levels of stress is a useful trait as a leader, but is also relative to the demands of the organization and situational factors. Greater demands, more intense pressures and hostile climates demand greater adjustment. Leaders must take responsibility and take the brunt of consequences, which requires emotional stability. A strategist must be able to overcome their own emotional (in)stability and focus on the values and strategy of the organization. Those with high adjustment are very resilient to stress while those with low adjustment are more affected by potential difficulties they face at work.

3 **Curiosity.** Curiosity is essential for strategy: the desire to learn and explore information is foundational for the strategist. Good strategy is rooted in a rich understanding of the company, the people in it, and what is going on outside of the organization. Continual learning informs the top-down strategy, helps to discover successful emergent strategy and to make informed decisions. It is difficult to develop a strategic understanding of any issue or company without intellectual curiosity. Those with high curiosity like new methods and ideas; those with lower curiosity tend to stick to tried-and-true methods.

4 **Risk Approach.** Risk approach is how willing someone is to confront and solve difficult situations. The leader as a strategist must have the courage to explain why strategy is important, even in the face of opposition. They must have the fortitude to stand by and explain their own values. Those with higher risk approach have a more proactive approach to dealing with problems whereas those with lower risk approach tend to have more reactive, instinctual responses.

5 **Ambiguity acceptance.** Ambiguity acceptance is how someone approaches uncertainty and complexity. The oversimplified solutions are often the most appealing and the least successful. Those with high ambiguity

acceptance seek out more information, even when there are conflicting opinions. Leaders must have the capacity to listen to unpopular or dissenting opinions, and those with low ambiguity acceptance have little tolerance for vagaries or complexity. Good strategy cannot form without understanding of complex issues. Simple, unambiguous and insincere solutions are frequently peddled by toxic leaders. Those with higher ambiguity acceptance thrive in complex environments whereas those with lower ambiguity acceptance prefer clear-cut answers and stable working environments.

6 Competitiveness. Competitiveness is instrumental, but in moderation. Useful competitiveness focuses on the success of the organization, and competitive advantage of teams, departments and the company. The moderately and adaptively competitive leader can channel their desire to succeed into realistic objectives. The hypercompetitive leader wants to be seen as the success of the organization, whereas the uncompetitive leader may have difficulty focusing on strategic advantages and pursuing opportunities. Those with lower competitiveness take a more collaborative approach.

Conclusion

Good leaders have the same traits across industries, and while technology and the economy change, organizations still need a strong, stable, visionary leader who models and lives the organizational culture. In some sectors, like the start-up tech sector, some leaders seem to be successful with style over substance. But without the substance and a viable business and effective leadership team, the company is probably headed for disaster.

References

Hull, J (2016) How your leadership has to change as your startup scales, *Harvard Business Review*, 20 May

Illing, S (2017) Uber and the problem of Silicon Valley's bro culture, *Vox*, 28 February. Available at: https://www.vox.com/conversations/2017/ 2/28/14726004/uber-susan-fowler-travis-kalanick-sexism-silicon-valley

Lyons, D (2017) Jerks and the start-ups they ruin, *New York Times*, 1 April. Available at: https://www.nytimes.com/2017/04/01/opinion/sunday/jerks-and-the-start-ups-they-ruin.html

MacRae, I and Furnham, A (2014) *High Potential: How to spot manage and develop talented people at work*, Bloomsbury, London

Minter, H (2017) How to tackle bro-culture in startups, *Guardian*, 13 March. Available at: https://www.theguardian.com/careers/2017/mar/13/sexism-tech-startups-women-workplace

Sorcher, S (2013) How the military's 'Bro' culture turns women into targets, *The Atlantic*, 9 September. Available at: https://www.theatlantic.com/national/archive/2013/09/how-the-militarys-bro-culture-turns-women-into-targets/279460/

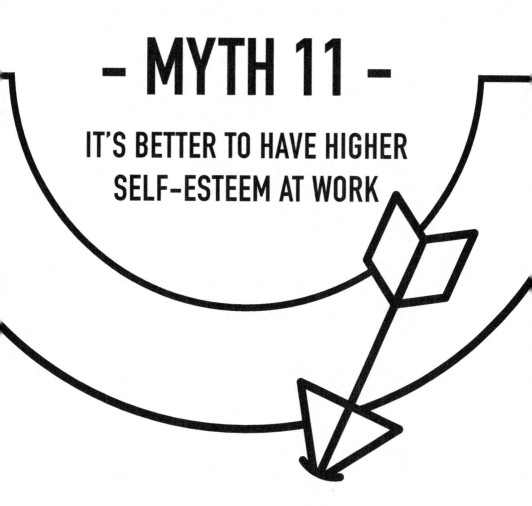

- MYTH 11 -

IT'S BETTER TO HAVE HIGHER SELF-ESTEEM AT WORK

*The importance of self-esteem and its effects on performance at work
are not insignificant, but are largely exaggerated.*

Introduction

Self-esteem is a sense of belief or confidence in one's own abilities. Higher
self-esteem is generally thought to be a good thing, and an asset in the workplace. It's an important topic for managers, HR departments and indeed
anyone who works with other people. Self-esteem highly influences how
people behave with their colleagues, how confident they are with their work
and can have a great deal of influence on how workers present themselves.

It is true that a host of problems can come with having low self-esteem at
work. Those with lower self-esteem tend to be more cautious, self-conscious,

socially withdrawn, struggle to take risks and can have interpersonal problems. Those with very low self-esteem may be too embarrassed to make use of their abilities and talents at work. Being cautious, avoidant and self-conscious is linked to social and interpersonal problems. Without self-confidence, people can spend more time doubting the quality of their own work, or worrying about how their colleagues will view them, than being productive. Low self-esteem has been linked with all sorts of problems including leadership derailment, work failure, interpersonal conflict, difficulty finding work and challenges with maintaining quality standards.

The research on low self-esteem led to a natural investigation of the benefits of higher self-esteem. Improving self-esteem in everyone from children and adolescents to adult workers can help to mitigate some of the problems mentioned above. However, some would say it has been taken too far.

The self-esteem movement

'There are no limits to what you can achieve if you put your mind to it', is a common message. School children are told they can achieve anything if they work hard enough for it and want it enough. Motivational speakers are brought in to motivate workers, supposedly inspiring them to work harder, be more productive and achieve their 'full' potential.

The rapid rise of the self-esteem movement has made it popular to focus training programmes, education and projects on increasing people's self-confidence. Believe in yourself and you'll succeed, and some people seem to believe self-confidence is enough to get ahead. For some it is: over-confidence and bluster sometimes work. Often people are impressed by others' self-confidence and (occasionally delusional) capacity to promise to fix the world's problems, to succeed in unprecedented ways. High promises and charm can be useful, especially in business, but overconfidence can be a swift path to failure.

Others have criticized the self-esteem movement. It starts early in schools and is for example illustrated in competitions where every child might get a participation award irrespective of their performance. It's an idea that doesn't always translate well into the working world. Not everyone gets the same reward just for showing up to work. Work is generally more merito-cratic, rewarding performance. You don't get a bonus for thinking you are the best performer; you get a bonus for actual performance.

It is easy to argue that the self-esteem pendulum has swung too far, that we're making people focus too much on confidence and less on performance.

There is absolutely some truth in this, but that does not mean the pendulum should swing too hard the other way, that we should be crushing all the hopes and dreams of the workforce until they are pliant but nervous wrecks.

Excessive self-esteem and narcissism

The most obvious risk with boosting self-esteem is that when it goes too far it can lead to arrogant, conceited, self-satisfied behaviour which is not beneficial or constructive in the workplace (Emler, 2005).

In his book *Confidence* (2014), Tomas Chamorro-Premuzic describes how self-esteem is seen to be useful, the key to success in life and business. While many people feel they are hindered by low confidence, they admire those who appear to be more confident and self-assured.

In *Confidence*, he shows us that high confidence can actually make people less likeable, less employable, and less successful in the long run. Lower levels of self-confidence can have an upside. Modesty, humility, being self-aware and being unpretentious can all be attractive qualities both in life and in work. Competent employees with lower self-esteem are more likely to under-promise and over-deliver. Employees with higher self-esteem are more likely to over-promise and under-deliver, particularly when their confidence exceeds their ability.

Similarly, it is important to try to distinguish between unhealthy narcissism which comes with being self-absorbed and vain, and genuine and appropriate high self-esteem. High self-esteem is healthier for those who have impressive abilities supported by a long track record.

The problem with narcissists (people who have chronic and excessively high self-esteem) is that they are extremely dependent on others to encourage them and validate their high opinion of themselves. They become very vulnerable because they are addicted to praise and affirmation from others. If they lose the praise they are dependent on at work, they become emotional or unhinged, although in many cases they could be said to have low self-esteem, which is why they depend so much on colleagues to maintain their artificial confidence.

Accurate self-evaluation

The essence of the argument is that we need to be accurate in self-evaluation about our competencies with a spirit of acceptance and realism. To be self-accepting we need to take responsibility for our actions. Hence there is a difference between authentic or genuine self-esteem and external or false self-esteem. The former is internal and under our control, the latter external and under the control of others, and may be insecure and fickle.

People need to be aware of their own capacity and limitations at work, which should align with their levels of self-esteem. Instead of boosting self-esteem, we should be focusing more on realistic levels of self-confidence at work. There is no point inflating the self-esteem of an incompetent employee; that is just setting them up for failure. It would (hypothetically) be possible to convince someone that they were a natural swimmer, and that if they just put their mind to it they could win against Olympic swimmers. But if they build up the confidence and never learn to swim then they will sink.

Talent competitions often make use of this problem for humorous purposes or to exasperate audiences. If you believe in yourself and just want it hard enough, you should be able to win, right? Wrong. Your talent needs to match.

The upside of failure

Self-esteem is more related to the risks we are willing to take than our likelihood to succeed or fail. In development, learning how to fail is more important than self-esteem or success.

Everyone will make mistakes and fail at various times throughout their life and career, and the consequences and implications will vary greatly. Mistakes happen, and the most successful, effective workers have the capacity to deal with mistakes and learn from failure.

There are various arguments in favour of focusing on failure. First, it helps understanding. Errors illustrate underlying principles clearly. Second, errors are seriously memorable; people tend not to repeat errors if they are aware of the cause and the effect of them, and can reflect upon them in a supervised environment. Third, errors underline the message of thinking before acting, of being attentive, being 'all there'. This helps to concentrate the mind, identify problems and generate sensible solutions.

Irrespective of self-confidence levels, learning how to deal with failure is essential. High-potential, successful people make mistakes and learn not to make the same mistake twice. Or they learn how to prevent the problem in the future. They become even more capable of dealing with future problems. Lower-potential employees are more likely to make the same mistake repeatedly because they either do not take responsibility for their part, or do not understand why things are going badly.

Excessive self-esteem can be a barrier to learning from failure. People who are overconfident in their abilities can have more difficulty taking responsibility for failure. They may have such inflated levels of self-esteem that they cannot imagine how a mistake could have possibly been their fault – they blame others or outside conditions without reflecting on what they might have done wrong.

Those with lower self-esteem may have trouble learning to fail for different reasons. They may not have the confidence to try new challenges or opportunities, being too fearful of failure. Or they may worry too much about what other people think of their mistakes to pick themselves up after failure, learn how to deal with it and move on to the next challenge.

The importance of self-esteem and its effects on performance at work are not insignificant, but are largely exaggerated.

Conclusion

Self-esteem is generally healthy and an asset to productivity at work when it aligns with abilities. While self-esteem can be useful, excessively high self-esteem can cause interpersonal conflict and performance issues. Low self-esteem, conversely and contrary to popular opinion, is not always a problem.

Those with self-awareness, who are neither too humble nor too braggadocious about their talents and abilities, will be most successful. Paradoxically, it can be extremely unwise and unhealthy to concentrate on boosting self-esteem when it is not in alignment with actual capabilities.

References and further reading

Baumeister, R et al (2003) Does high self-esteem cause better performance, interpersonal success, happiness and healthier lifestyles? *Psychological Science in the Public Interest*, **4**, pp 1–44

Campbell, W (2001) Is narcissism really so bad? *Psychological Inquiry*, **12**, pp 214–16

Chamorro-Premuzic, T (2014) *Confidence*, Hudson Street Press, New York

Crocker, J and Wolfe, C (2001) Contingencies of self-worth, *Psychologist Review*, **108**, pp 593–623

Emler, N (2005) *The costs and causes of low self-esteem*, unpublished paper, London School of Economics

Otway, L and Vignoles, V (2006) Narcissism and childhood recollections, *Personality and Social Psychology Bulletin*, 32, pp 104–16

Twenge, J (2006) *Generation Me*, Free Press, New York

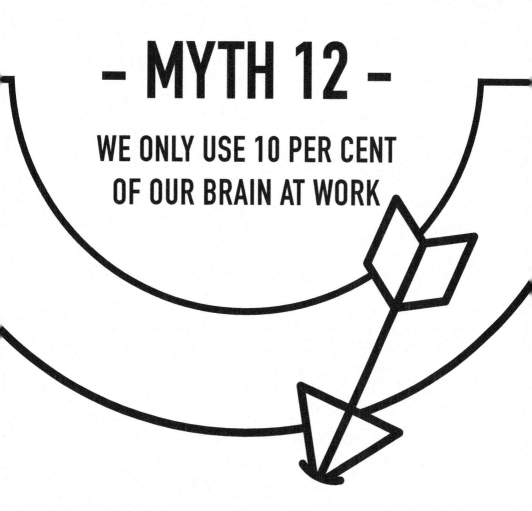

– MYTH 12 –

WE ONLY USE 10 PER CENT OF OUR BRAIN AT WORK

*It's not that humans have some untapped capacity in the brain –
all of the brain is used but for different purposes and at different times.*

Introduction

Imagine if everyone could work 10 times harder, be 10 times more intel-ligent, empathetic, analytic or organized. There is an enduring myth that humans only use 10 per cent of their brains and the rest is essentially room for growth.

It's one of the more ridiculous myths that is continually perpetuated in the workplace and in popular culture. The science fiction film *Lucy* (2014) uses this as a major plot point, when Scarlett Johannson's character is forced to take drugs that enable her to use the supposedly unused 90 per cent of her brain. It's a fiction that imagines that tapping into the purportedly unused 90 per cent can create superhuman powers of thinking, analysis and behaviour.

Work futurists love the idea that there is a quick solution or an easy short-cut to increasing performance or ability. Psychologists and physicians find the idea laughable and have trouble understanding why the myth continues to be perpetuated.

The biological argument

Barry Beyerstein (1999) at Simon Fraser University provided a nice analysis debunking the 10 per cent of the brain myth almost two decades ago, but it doesn't seem to have killed the myth. There are more problems with this myth than there is room for in this chapter. But one of the strongest arguments is that it is biologically and evolutionarily nonsensical. The brain is by far the most demanding organ on the body's resources, using about 20 per cent. Why would such a powerful organ be so inefficient, leaving 90 per cent unused? It's not that humans have some untapped capacity in the brain – all of the brain is used but for different purposes and at different times.

There have been numerous biological studies that could confirm or deny the 10 per cent myth and the evidence overwhelmingly shows that the brain already uses its full capacity. Metabolic studies, microstructural analysis and work on neural disease provide no support for the 10 per cent myth, which seems to have originated in the self-improvement industry.

Brain-imaging technology also shows that, even during sleep, there are no completely silent areas in the brain. Next, in the extensive examination of brain functioning and specialty localization, no one has detected the silent 90 per cent that is not used.

Another argument should illustrate the point by considering what happens when part of the brain is removed. Surely if only 10 per cent of the human brain is used, then the other 90 per cent could be removed without much worry. Slick salespeople who boast about 90 per cent increased brain capacity are largely overstating their case.

Next, given the process of natural selection, it seems improbable that scarce resources would be wasted to produce and maintain an underutilized organ.

The importance of attention

The reality is the human brain has a huge capacity for thought, attention and analysis but can't do everything at once. Imagine a situation at work where you could make full use of all of your senses while thinking about every single task and responsibility. Try it right now. Feel the temperature of the air on your skin. Take a deep breath through your nose and see what you can smell. Listen to every sound that is going on around you no matter how noisy or subtle. Think about what you had for breakfast this morning and the first conversation you had at work today. Think about what you need to do today, this week, and over the next month. Consider your career goals and what you would like to accomplish at work in the coming year, and in 10 years' time. Think about what your colleagues are working on and what they would like to accomplish, and then think about how that aligns with your own career goals.

It's not possible. One of the strengths of the human brain is actually its ability to focus on certain details and block out excessive information. It's called attention. The brain is also astoundingly adaptable in its ability to use and process many different types of information and use it to be adaptable, intelligent and learn and improve at work.

Using the example of the film mentioned in the introduction, if your employer gave you a pill that forced you to use 100 per cent of your brain at every moment (assuming it was possible) it wouldn't be empowering or helpful – it would be overwhelming and terrifying. There would be a constant barrage of unfiltered information at rapid speeds that would be impossible to focus on. Imagine watching CNN and listening to nine different talk radio stations at the same time.

Intelligence and performance at work rely on the ability to filter and process information, focus on specific tasks and use a personally curated set of information.

Gains in the workplace

It is appealing to think that the majority of our brain is unused, and there is a huge untapped potential to improve. Imagine increasing productivity, performance and profitability tenfold. It's unfortunate that it's little more than a fantasy with no basis in fact.

The truth about what psychologists have learned from neuroscientific research is that people can improve. Learning and development does affect the brain, but in subtle and cumulative ways. If you want to improve performance in the workplace, the path is much more difficult than taking a magic pill or potion to become better overnight. Like an athlete training their body and developing technique, practice and training improves performance. The brain, like the body, does have the capacity to improve but the untapped potential is not some sort of vacant space waiting to be filled.

Memory, one of the brain's important functions, is a good example of this. There isn't a secret cache of memory hiding in your brain. There is, however, the capacity to learn information and build up skills and expertise by reading and practising. Improving performance isn't about discovering some secret cache of talent. It's about hard work, learning, training and development.

Conclusion

It seems likely that some early investigations (probably optimistic) estimating that researchers only know what 10 per cent of the brain does may have been misinterpreted as an assertion that we normally only use 10 per cent of it. The concept of a nice, unused spare bedroom to fall back on or to use as needed is loved by pop psychologists promising to improve performance tenfold. And while it is a popular trope in science fiction, it remains solely in the domain of fiction, not science.

References

Beyerstein, B (1999) Whence cometh the myth that we only use ten percent of our brains? In *Mind-myths: Exploring everyday mysteries of the mind and brain*, ed S D Sala, John Wiley and Sons, New York

Lucy (2014) Directed by Luc Besson [film]

- MYTH 13 -

MAKING WORKPLACES SUSTAINABLE IS A BURDEN

Companies would be wise to adopt and implement environmental policies to perform well and outperform their outdated competitors who ignore climate change and the relevant policies.

Introduction

Environmental regulations, efforts and mandates to make businesses more environmentally friendly are seen as a burden and a cost to most businesses. Climate change is no longer being disputed in the scientific community (IPCC, 2014) and its potential effects are more of a political debate than a scientific one (Funk and Kennedy, 2016).

The highly respected international research and policy-making group, the Organization for Economic Co-operation and Development (OECD), says that environmental regulations have a direct impact on the economy and 'Likely they impact well beyond the sectors directly concerned, hampering productivity growth, as shown for other product market regulations' (Koźluk, 2014). Yet the story is not that simple, and even an organization that so often prioritizes free markets and economic growth goes on to say that 'The burdens of environmental policies are not related to their actual stringency, indicating that ambitious environmental targets can be pursued in ways that are more (or less) friendly to competition' (Koźluk, 2014). In other words, sustainable workplaces or environmental regulations can be, but aren't necessarily a problem for businesses.

The question, irrespective of ideology is: are sustainable policies and legislation good or bad for workplaces?

Effects on people and profitability

Let's put aside the discussion of receding glaciers, rising sea levels, ocean acidification and increased severe weather events. What's the potential effect of global climate change on the workplace? Delmas and Pekovic (2012) found that companies that voluntarily implemented environmentally friendly policies had employees that were, on average, 16 per cent more productive. The authors said they were surprised by how stark the differences were and by how much more productive the environmentally focused organizations were (Hewitt, 2012).

Of course, implementing environmentally friendly practices in the workplace rarely occurs in isolation. The practices are typically part of a 'virtuous cycle' that is often part of education and training initiatives to get their employees to implement environmentally friendly policies. It usually comes from larger initiatives to make the workplace a better place for its workers, as well as reducing the company's negative environmental impacts.

Implementing better HR policy, along with greener work policies, helps to attract people who think their workplace surroundings, as well as the overall environment, are important and should be improved (Zokaei, 2013; Dumont, Shen and Deng, 2016). Naturally, if a company is seen as a market leader in ethical and strong environmental initiatives it has an opportunity to attract the best, brightest and most motivated to do good and to do well in the workplace (Dumont, Shen and Deng, 2016).

Research published in the *Harvard Business Review* (Haanaes et al, 2013) looked at over 100 companies around the world worth between US $25 million and US $5 billion and found that companies that embraced environmentally sustainable practices reduced costs, thus increasing profit and improving productivity. A good example is from DuPoint (Zokaei, 2013), a company with over US $25 billion in annual revenue. In 2000, they decided to reduce their CO_2 emissions by 65 per cent by 2010. In only seven years, the policy was saving them US $2.2 billion every year in energy efficiency. Of course, changing policies takes hard work and dedication, but the effects are not just good for the environment – they are good for business.

This chapter is not going to go into a detailed moralistic argument about why companies should reduce their environmental impact or be more resilient to climate change – that argument has already been made extensively elsewhere (see Worldwatch Institute, 2012, 2016, 2017, for example). There is a strong business case to be made for making workplaces environmentally sustainable.

Changing environmental policy in a company takes time, effort and investment by the people in the company – much like any policy, whether it's HR, legal or ethical. But it is a step worth taking to reduce costs, and improve profitability and productivity. Unlike some environmental campaigners, we are not advocating for centrally controlled command economies. Not all companies can be forced to be at the cutting edge of making workplaces more sustainable. The organizations that do implement the more innovative sustainability policies have the opportunity to be more competitive and productive. Even companies that have, at times, been seen to be behind the curve are now advocates for sustainable policy and business practice. While innovators like Google, Microsoft, Facebook, Apple and Amazon have backed sustainable policy, other advocates may seem more surprising. Even energy companies like Exxon and Shell, along with coal giants Peabody Energy and Murray Energy have advocated for sustainable policies (Victor, 2017). Companies would be wise to adopt and implement environmental policies to perform well and outperform their outdated competitors who ignore climate change and the relevant policies.

CASE STUDY Jackson Family Wines

Climate-controlled offices with cappuccino machines, on-site gyms or cafeterias might seem to be far removed from the changes in climate. Yet every business and office will have to adapt in its own way, based on the unique conditions and opportunities in the business. An interesting and unique example of making a workplace and a business sustainable can be found in California's wine industry (Gelles, 2017). This industry is on the frontlines of collision between changing climate and ambitions to react to these changes and develop long-term resilience for businesses.

We use this example because it highlights a particular case from a specific industry and looks at how they are adapting to climate change and implementing sustainable policies. That's not to say the sustainable activities in this example can be applied to every workplace, but different companies must be innovative and adaptive in the context of their particular industry. There is no 10-point checklist that can future-proof every single company. What's more important is to have a mindset and openness to encouraging sustainability in the workplace. Then take the lesson of being open and innovative and come up with solutions that apply to the specific workplace, its environmental impact, vulnerabilities and opportunities.

The problem for the wine industry in California is that warmer temperatures mean grapes are ripening earlier than usual, and new pests are moving in. The nights are warmer than they used to be and water is becoming more and more scarce. A vineyard isn't a typical office workplace, because much of the work is done out of doors, is active and physical, and workers are exposed to the elements and any changes in climate.

Jackson Family Wines (Gelles, 2017) have come up with some innovative and rather charming ways to make their workplace more environmentally friendly. For example, to deal in an environmental friendly way with the new pests that are drawn to the warmer winters, they have moved in 68 barn owls to take care of the small mammals that overpopulate the vineyards, and a falconer to release a falcon every day to scare away the small birds and crows that would eat the fruit on the vine. Working with birds of prey removes the environmental impact that would come from pesticides or similar methods. And barn owls don't need to be paid a minimum wage, or ask for maternity leave or contributions to retirement plans. Falcons are solitary birds, so tend not to have issues with collective bargaining rights or organized labour.

The important point to take from this study is that there is no quick and easy checklist to being innovative, no necessarily simple or easy solutions. You can be more creative than just printing fewer documents and turning the lights off in empty rooms. It is important and necessary to think of innovative solutions that are unique and specific to the business and its interaction with the environment. Obviously, it is not easy, and not every office would benefit from a fleet of hawks and owls, but this case study illustrates how it is possible to be more environmentally friendly, to adapt to climate change and to develop ideas that make the business more successful, more viable, and more profitable in the long term.

Conclusion

Changes in the natural environment and climate change are an increasing threat to businesses of all types, and will continue to increase with the severity and frequency of severe weather events. That said, it is possible to consider the challenges from climate change as an opportunity, not just a threat. Businesses adopting environmentally friendly practices and policies have clearly demonstrated that this approach can reduce costs, and increase productivity and profitability. Making workplaces sustainable should be seen as a challenge and an opportunity, not a burden. Like with any new wave of technology and innovation, businesses that can adapt and improve will thrive. The businesses that act like the proverbial frog in a pot of boiling water, ignorant to the changes in their environment, who cannot innovate or change with their business environment, will ultimately be the ones who are saddled with the burden of being uncompetitive.

References and further reading

Delmas, M A and Pekovic, S (2012) Environmental standards and labor productivity: understanding the mechanisms that sustain sustainability, *Journal of Organizational Behavior*, **34** (2), pp 230–52

Dumont, J, Shen, J and Deng, X (2016) Effects of green HRM practices on employee workplace green behaviour: the role of psychological green climate, *Human Resource Management*, 10 June

Funk, C and Kennedy, B (2016) The politics of climate, *Pew Research Centre*. Available at: http://www.pewinternet.org/2016/10/04/the-politics-of-climate/

Gelles, D (2017) Falcons, drones, data: a winery battles climate change, *New York Times*, 5 January. Available at: https://www.nytimes.com/2017/01/05/business/california-wine-climate-change.html

Haanaes, K et al (2013) Making sustainability profitable, *Harvard Business Review*, March

Hewitt, A (2012) Employees at 'green' companies are significantly more productive, study finds. *UCLA Newsroom*. Available at: http://newsroom.ucla.edu/releases/study-certified-green-companies-238203

Intergovernmental Panel on Climate Change (IPCC) (2014) Climate change 2014 synthesis report summary for policymakers, *IPCC*. Available at: https://www.ipcc.ch/report/ar5/syr

Kitching, J (2006) A burden on business? Reviewing the evidence base on regulation and small business performance, *Environment and Planning C: Government and planning*, **26** (6), pp 799–814

Koźluk, T (2014) The indicators of the economic burdens of environmental policy design - results from the OECD Questionnaire, OECD Working Papers No 1178, Organization for Economic Cooperation and Development

Victor, D (2017) 'Climate change is real': Many US companies lament Paris Accord exit, *New York Times*, 1 June. Available at: https://www.nytimes.com/2017/06/01/business/climate-change-tesla-corporations-paris-accord.html

Worldwatch Institute (2012) *State of the World 2012: Moving toward sustainable prosperity*, Island Press, London

Worldwatch Institute (2016) *Can a City be Sustainable? State of the World (2016)*, Island Press, London

Worldwatch Institute (2017) *EarthEd: Rethinking Education on a Changing Planet: State of the World 2017*, Island Press, London

Zokaei, K (2013) Environmentally friendly business is profitable business, *Guardian*, 14 October. Available at: https://www.theguardian.com/sustainable-business/environmentally-friendly-sustainable-business-profitable

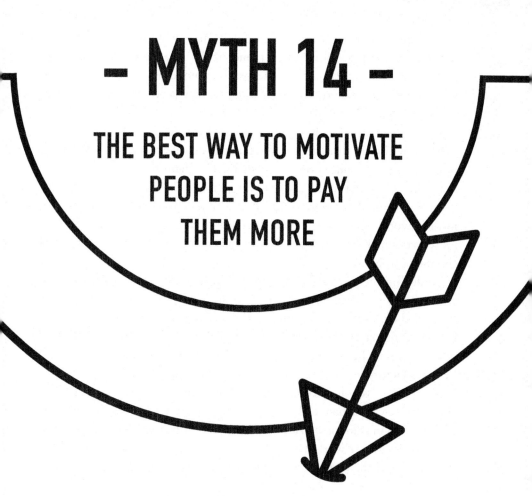

- MYTH 14 -

THE BEST WAY TO MOTIVATE PEOPLE IS TO PAY THEM MORE

Money is most effective as a tool to attract and retain talent, but in the workplace employees need to be motivated by far more than just their paycheck.

Introduction

People work for pay, and pay is a fundamental component of almost any job. Whether it's a salary, hourly wage, commission, or pay for performance, all work shares a common reward: money. Much is made of intrinsic motivation, need for autonomy and independence and all the other reasons people work and enjoy their work. Yet it is impossible to get past the fact that people do work for money.

But does money really motivate people? Can pay motivate some workers but not others? How powerful is money really in affecting motivation or performance at work? Some would argue that money is not the best motivator, like in the *Forbes* article, tersely titled 'Money is not the best motivator' (Katzenbach and Khan, 2010).

However, money does have some effect in the workplace. Financial incentives are useful for attracting and retaining top talent, but less effective at motivating people once you've got them. The main thing to remember is that money is important, but day to day it is not the most important motivator. People need autonomy and a degree of independence to be motivated in their work. Many work for the respect of their peers or colleagues, or for a communal or greater good. Money is not a substitute for that, but it certainly can be complementary.

Studies on pay and job satisfaction indicate there is a relationship between pay and job satisfaction, but it is modest at best. A thorough review by Judge and colleagues (2010) found about 15 per cent overlap between pay and job satisfaction. This is enough to say that pay has a limited effect on job satisfaction, but the vast majority of job satisfaction must be explained by other factors.

The basic psychology of money would say that behaviour can be influenced by rewards, financial or otherwise. Pay can more easily influence behaviour than emotions, so a person can be incentivized to complete a task, work for longer, or work more quickly but that does not necessarily mean they will enjoy the work or be satisfied in it.

Reasons why money motivates (or doesn't)

Money can be a powerful motivator, but the research and evidence consistently shows that money can only provide happiness up to a point. Money is better at combating unhappiness (dealing with problems, avoiding difficulties) than actually making people more motivated or satisfied with their work. Poverty is often tied to unhappiness because there are a wide range of relatively straightforward day-to-day problems a bit of money can make easier. When a laptop breaks or there is added personal expense to a business trip, when there is an added monthly expense or a financial hardship, it creates stress that spills over into the person's work life and environment. A bit of money can easily solve these problems, but beyond relieving day-to-day hassles, money has little power to actually make people more satisfied at work.

Beyond average income levels, money cannot do very much to make people happier, and there are four main reasons why:

1 **Adaptation.** Anything from finding a surprise bit of money in your pocket to a seasonal bonus or a lottery win can cause temporary motivation, drive and excitement. A windfall of cash leads to a brief or momentary period of excitement that feels good. But it's not the same as internal motivation to do a better job and any new amount of money, be it £10 or £10,000,000, is surprisingly easy to adjust to. It may change one's daily approach to spending, attitude to money at work or lifestyle spending habits, but it will not make employees any more motivated in the long term. Any amount of money is surprisingly easy to adapt to and once it becomes normal, its effect on motivation wears off.

2 **Comparison.** How rich is rich? The surprising answer is that almost no one really thinks they are 'rich'. The rich are people who make more money than you. Millionaires think billionaires are rich. Billionaires think oligarchs and multinational corporations are rich. No matter how much money you make, there will always be someone who is making more, who is richer than you. Promising to make employees 'rich' would be an elusive and ambiguous promise for any employer. Often the more money people make, the more aware they are of other people who are richer, more powerful or more influential than them. Wealth is a comparative sport where it is almost impossible to come out on top. Highly paid employees are rarely more or less motivated just by money, particularly when their colleagues are on a similar salary.

3 **Alternatives.** Money only goes so far and buys so many things. As one accumulates more money, and spends more time accumulating money, there seem to be more things that money can't buy. Extra vacation time, closer relationships with friends or colleagues, freedom from work and the responsibilities that come with greater income and work responsibilities all become scarcer commodities at the same time as personal wealth builds up. Oftentimes money seems less valuable as it becomes less useful in buying the scarcities and the things that seem truly valuable in life.

4 **Worry.** With greater wealth comes greater responsibility. There is only a limited set of problems that money can be used to solve. And the accumulation of wealth is often linked with concern about how best to save, invest, maintain and make best use of the wealth one is responsible for. Earning more at work can create anxiety about losing that high level of compensation, or create greater stress about the value of the annual bonus. Paradoxically, since money can help solve some problems, its

presence can shift the attention to other problems that are more difficult or impossible to solve, such as interpersonal conflict, family or health problems, and this can leave one feeling out of control or helpless when personal financial resources can't seem to solve the problems that seem the most important.

The pay-for-performance fable

Fleischer (2015) describes pay for performance as akin to a religious tenet in American culture and thus western work culture. Work hard, perform well, be productive and you will be compensated for the effort, ability and graft put into the work.

A pay-for-performance system means that money is tied to specific elements of performance or outcomes in the work. The number of widgets produced, the volume of sales, the overall performance of a department or entire company are the basis for how much money is paid. There is often an inherent competitiveness in these systems, when a limited reward pool is paid to the top performers.

The drawback of pay-for-performance systems is that they can encourage short-term thinking. Pay an employee for their immediate performance, give them quarterly or monthly rewards for their performance within that duration, and the system can drive people to focus on short-term gains and avoid long-term consequences.

It's rooted in the fable that Fleischer (2015) describes of leaders and employees having an overall focus on what's good for the company. He describes long-term loyalists whose job security, personal commitment and self-image are tied up within the company they are working for. Leaders deliver reward on short-term performance and assume that other motivators keep the person's long-term interests and loyalties committed to the company vision. This mindset can create competitiveness for pay and compensation in the workplace that shifts employee focus to making more money than colleagues instead of focusing on improving performance.

Pay for performance dominates the modern workplace, but it is not always sufficient to assume that pay can be the sole reward for performance and the rest will take care of itself. It is necessary to remember that paying for performance only rewards and encourages precisely the behaviour it is linked to. Pay is not enough to motivate people to long-term ethical and constructive work behaviour.

What money can't buy

As was previously mentioned, money has little ability to make people happier beyond basic, average national income levels. The value of money is a bit strange because we live in a world where people tend to overestimate the value of excessive wealth. People who make great fortunes quickly find that many of their problems, troubles and concerns cannot be solved financially.

To understand this, consider a piece of research conducted with individuals who had a net worth of US $25 million or more (Judge et al, 2010). As part of the research, these people were asked about their aspirations for themselves, their children and their world. The most common aspiration of these wealthy individuals actually had nothing to do with money: the most common aspiration was to be a good parent. They said their wealth helped in some ways, but was equally a concern. They worried that early access to wealth would demotivate their children and negatively affect how they developed independence. Very few said their main aspiration for their children was for them to become wealthy. This also holds true to the workplace. Money can solve or mitigate some problems, but it cannot resolve all problems or be a sole motivating force.

While greater income levels offer a wealth of options and choice, a wider range of options and availability of choice does not necessarily come with greater expertise or insight into making the right decisions. Often this puts more time pressures on the individual, putting pressure on how best to use those resources and how to allocate the most precious resource of time.

No matter how much money a person makes, there will always be things they still cannot purchase, and the most notable and most precious of those resources is time.

Conclusion

Money has little power to motivate people or make them happier beyond moderate levels of pay. Money is most effective as a tool to attract and retain talent, but in the workplace employees need to be motivated by far more than just their paycheck. It must be complemented by intrinsic motivators that drive people to work more effectively through enjoyment and engagement in their work. Motivators like autonomy, independence and the ability to innovate drive people to be more productive and more satisfied in their work.

References

Fleischer, V (2015) The executive paycheck myth, *New York Times*, 4 November. Available at: https://www.nytimes.com/2015/11/05/business/dealbook/the-executive-paycheck-myth.html

Judge, T A et al (2010) The relationship between pay and job satisfaction: a meta-analysis of the literature, *Journal of Vocational Behavior*, 77, pp 157–67

Katzenbach, J R and Khan, Z (2010) Money is not the best motivator, *Forbes*, 6 April. Available at: https://www.forbes.com/2010/04/06/money-motivation-pay-leadership-managing-employees.html

– MYTH 15 –

EMPLOYEES WHO WORK THE LONGEST HOURS ARE THE MOST VALUABLE PEOPLE

Productive and engaged workaholics are the exception – not the rule.

Introduction

Are the best employees those who put in many hours of overtime? Or should employees work a comfortable 30- or 35-hour week to be well rested, healthy and avoid overwork and burnout?

While most countries have settled into 21st-century idea of 30–40-hour average workweek, there has been a great deal of variation over time and today hours worked can vary greatly amongst workers. Of the developed countries, South Koreans work the most hours – 2,124 hours per year (averaging about 41 hours/week) – while Germans work about 26 hours per week (1,336 hours/year). The United States (32 hours/week), Canada

(33 hours/week) and the UK (34 hours/week) fall somewhere in the middle (OECD, 2016).

Of course, the history of working hours shows that people in many countries work fewer hours than their parents before them, and fewer still than their grandparents. This is not true of every country. However, in 1870, British workers worked about 53 hours per week and the Germans worked 62 hours per week. By 1950, British workers were working 41 hours per week and the Germans 46 hours (Lee, McCann and Messenger, 2007).

These hours are a rough approximation of weekly hours that do not account for factors like productivity, unions, labour laws, mechanization or type of work. Which is exactly why it is a good introduction to this myth: *are employees who work longer hours more valuable?*

The answer is, of course, it depends how the employees are spending those hours. For some, work is a tedious monotony of hours, days, weeks and decades. A dull or dreadful prelude to retirement. Others, who get meaning and enjoyment from their work, can relate to Noël Coward's idea that 'The only way to enjoy life is to work. Work is more fun than fun.' Of course, that greatly depends on what your work entails. Perhaps Noël Coward would have felt differently if he was a coal miner or rat catcher.

For some companies and organizations, a culture of presenteeism is the norm – the more time employees spend at work, the more valuable they are seen to be. Let's look at one example of how this can go wrong.

CASE STUDY   A culture of presenteeism

We spoke to an employee at a large London financial services company who requested to remain nameless. He is a young, 20-something worker in a graduate-level position. He earns substantially more than the average UK salary of £26,500, taking home far more after perks, bonuses and benefits.

The company culture expects employees to work 'hard' – equating hard work with long hours. Twelve-hour days, five or six days per week are the norm for this company culture. It is an extremely competitive culture, where workdays are turned into a marathon of presenteeism. Long workdays are the norm, so everyone in the office tries to outlast each other.

The company perks recognize, encourage and incentivize people to stay longer. Employees who are still in the office after 6pm are rewarded with a free dinner, ordered directly to the office. Employees who stay later than 8 pm will have the cost of their taxi ride home reimbursed. Often, beer, wine or harder alcoholic beverages appear out of desks or alongside the takeaway meals during these overtime hours.

Of course, these incentives do encourage the behaviour, but do little to improve performance. The employee we talked with said he rarely gets more than five or six hours of work done per day. Even though most people are spending 60 to 80 hours per week in the office, only about half that time is productive.

Typically, many people in this office return to work tired or hungover the following day. That's an hour or two of recovery, staring mindlessly at e-mails and checking social media or the news. A few hours of work, then lunch. Then a quick slog of work before the evening approaches. Nearing 4pm it only takes two hours of procrastination to get the free dinner. After a long time of eating dinner at the desk and protracted conversations about projects and office politics, it's not too much longer to stay for the free taxi ride home. When this type of culture is normalized it is because of *social contagion.* Everyone behaves that way, so it seems quite normal to everyone in that situation.

Generously rewarding hours worked, and creating a culture where long hours are seen as mandatory, can easily create a culture of presenteeism that does little to improve productivity and neglects the fact that just because workers are in the office does not mean any work is getting done.

When long hours work (and don't)

The effectiveness of working long (or short) hours depends, of course, on the nature of work. The job demands–resources model of work is a relatively straightforward explanation of how this works (Bakker and Demerouti, 2007). It is a classic four-box model that explains work along two continua. It explains productivity along the lines of two main dimensions. The first dimension is job resources, which are the psychological and material resources people get from their work. The second dimension explains the demands and strains of the work.

Table 15.1 below shows how the different dimensions interact. The main point is that people are most engaged and satisfied when their work is challenging but within their capacity and when they have sufficient resources to complete the work well. This means long hours might be appropriate for some people, but personal resources do limit the amount of time people can realistically work without succumbing to exhaustion and burnout. Conversely, simple jobs with no challenge and no support can be the most boring, disengaging types of work.

Table 15.1 Job resources and job demands continua

		Job resources	
		High	**Low**
Job demands	**High**	The work is challenging, exciting and rewarding. Think successful entrepreneur, inventor or leader.	The job is demanding and is impossible or inordinately stressful. Think salesperson trying to sell terrible product, civil service trying to deliver better service with budget cuts.
	Low	The work is easily achievable but boring or unfulfilling. Think menial summer job for bright student.	The work is simplistic and entirely unfulfilling. Think George Orwell writing product descriptions for children's toys.

Job demands are all the things that are required from the work. These can be physical or psychological strains, social requirements and any necessary skills, abilities or knowledge. Job resources are essentially benefits and supports that the job provides. These can be personal fulfilment, career development, excitement, enjoyment, positive interactions with others or any other benefits.

The best jobs, often where long hours can be productive and enjoyable, are the jobs that are challenging and demanding but the employee has the capacity to do well. They can make use of their talents and stretch their abilities within realistic limits. The worst jobs are often those which are not demanding, offer no resources to the employee and do not make use of their talents.

Fatigue damages productivity as much as intoxication

Everyone likely experiences fatigue at work in one way or another, for one reason or another. It could be an enjoyable weekend where sleep was sacrificed at the expense of fun. It could be difficulty falling asleep or staying asleep at night. One might have noisy neighbours or snoring partners as roommates. There are many reasons people might become fatigued outside of work, but often work can be the cause of fatigue.

Overwork, strain and stress are very common reasons that people lose sleep and there are equally as many reasons someone's job could prevent them from sleeping. Maybe they have to be in the office for long hours, or perhaps they keep their work phone next to their bed at night and it rings, buzzes and vibrates at all hours of the day or night. Looming deadlines, performance reviews, conflict at work or tenuous working situations can all be stressful and damaging to sleep patterns.

Being tired at work is not just being sleepy; recent studies show that fatigue is actually damaging to performance, in many different ways. Fatigue and driving research has found that being tired behind the wheel is equally as dangerous as being over the drink-driving limit (Alleyne, 2011). Yet it is difficult to accurately measure tiredness in the same way as measuring alcohol intoxication. The effects are clear though: people who are tired, whether it is behind the wheel or in the workplace, have reduced performance (Williamson and Feyer, 2000).

Although levels of sleep and fatigue are difficult to measure, some organizations have realized how important it is to be well rested. The consequences of making mistakes due to fatigue may be minor in some organizations and more severe in others. The US Army invested US $18 million over 12 years to develop a model and measure of fatigue in the workplace (Clay, 2013).

Employee fatigue is an essential consideration in the workplace. There will be times and businesses or types of work where people may have to work long hours. Busy seasons, client demands, crises in the workplace or unexpected circumstances may all necessitate certain employees to work for longer than would typically be necessary for short or long periods of time. This may be unavoidable. However, employees should not be expected or encouraged to work excessively long hours when not necessary – it is more likely to diminish performance than increase productivity.

What you get from work

Victorian art critic and social thinker John Ruskin (Ruskin, 1985) was a strong proponent of work, believing the value of work was not what you *got* from it, but what you *became* from it. This idea is just as relevant now. Of course, if you're becoming a grumpy, burnt-out cynical bundle of nerves, perhaps what you're getting from work is not ideal.

Overworking employees beyond their individual capacity or ability, or stretching them beyond the limits of their job resources, often reduces productivity, increases sick leave and creates a host of problems (MacRae and Furnham, 2017). Yet stretch assignments, challenges, and longer workdays for the engaged, motivated and capable employees can enrich and improve experience and performance at work.

Conclusion

Long working hours for the sake of long working hours are worse than pointless. They are counterproductive and can make it difficult to see which employees are actually the most productive and valuable workers. Long hours are not right for everyone, but that is not to say they should be prohibited. Those who get a great deal out of their work, enjoy it and work productively for long hours are certainly valuable employees. But these productive and engaged workaholics are the exception – not the rule.

References

Alleyne, R (2011) Being tired behind the wheel is as bad as being drunk, *Telegraph*, 11 January. Available at: http://www.telegraph.co.uk/motoring/news/8269657/Being-tired-behind-the-wheel-as-bad-as-being-drunk.html

Bakker, A B and Demerouti, E (2007) The Job Demands–Resources model: state of the art, *Journal of Managerial Psychology*, **22**, pp 309–28

Clay, K (2013) Didn't get enough sleep? You might as well be drunk, *Forbes*, 4 September. Available at: https://www.forbes.com/sites/kellyclay/2013/09/04/didnt-get-enough-sleep-you-might-as-well-be-drunk/#247c7cbc10e2

Lee, S, McCann, D and Messenger, J C (2007) *Working Time Around the World: Trends in working hours, laws and policies in a global perspective*, Routledge, New York

MacRae, I and Furnham, A (2017) *Motivation and Performance: A guide to motivating a diverse workforce*, Kogan Page, London

Organization for Economic Cooperation and Development (OECD) (2016) Hours worked (indicator), OECD. Available at: http://www.oecd-ilibrary.org/employment/hours-worked/indicator/english_47be1c78-en

Ruskin, J (1860/1985) *Unto This Last and Other Writings*, Penguin, London

Williamson, A and Feyer, A (2000) Moderate sleep deprivation produces impairments in cognitive and motor performance equivalent to legally prescribed levels of alcohol intoxication, *Occupational & Environmental Medicine*, **57** (10), pp 645–55

- MYTH 16 -

PEOPLE SHOULD RETIRE AT 65

A retirement age of 65 is obsolete in the modern economy because there are so many different options for working later (as well as earlier) in life.

Introduction

Retirement at 65 has been a legal and cultural norm in many western countries for much of the 20th century, but it is rapidly disappearing. In the United States, the Social Security Act of 1935 legally established the retirement age of 65 (it should be noted, the average life expectancy for American men was 58 in that year). In the UK, mandatory retirement has never been a legal requirement but has been aligned with the pensionable age of 65 (Wunsch and Raman, 2010). However, mandatory retirement at age 65 became legally prohibited in 2011.

It should be noted that there are many different factors to consider in the context of retirement age, not least of which is average lifespans. Men in Glasgow live, on average, for 73 years while men in East Dorset can expect to live to about 83 (ONS, 2014). Men in Minnesota have a life expectancy five years longer than men in Mississippi, while women in Hawaii live seven years longer than those in Mississippi (CDC, 2015). Workers in Minnesota and East Dorset get 5 and 10 years more retirement years, which may be seen as a blessing or a curse, depending on your view of living in Dorset or Minnesota. If the retirement age is set at a mandatory 65, why should some people be required to spend a much greater proportion of their life working, while others are forced out of work when they are happy, healthy and want to continue with their job?

The goal of this chapter is not to argue that people should be required to work for longer, and we would not argue that 40+ years of hard work, paying taxes and contributing to a pension shouldn't be enough to enjoy retirement. But the argument is that if people are happy and healthy at work, if they enjoy their job and want to continue, why should a well-qualified and talented worker be required to stop working when they don't want to?

Health and retirement

The research on health and retirement is mixed at best. In a thorough analysis of long-term studies of health and retirement, van der Heide and colleagues (2013) found some evidence that mental health does improve after retirement. Yet while some studies found benefits of retirement for mental and physical health, other research indicated the reverse was true.

It has been suggested that the type and nature of retirement is responsible for positive or negative effects (van der Heide et al, 2013). When retirement means leaving behind stressful, difficult jobs, it can be joyful. When retirement is beyond the control of the retiree, it can be a stressful or difficult experience. For people who enjoy their jobs, finding meaning and satisfaction in their work, retirement may be a negative experience.

A case study on (not) retiring

To discuss retirement (and not retiring) we talked with Nicholas Parsons, actor and comedy performer, and host of BBC Radio 4's *Just a Minute*, who was born in 1923. He has been working for 75 years and sees no point in quitting.

He happily discusses how his work keeps him sharp, interested and engaged. In the Radio 4 comedy game show, he monitors contestants who compete to speak continuously for one minute without hesitation, repetition or deviation. Not an easy task to follow as a listener, let alone having the responsibility for controlling and interpreting the rules.

Nicholas Parsons says he can't imagine retiring because he loves the work, and working is just part of the profession. He mentions the requirements of the work, saying, 'The profession I'm in is the most fragile and difficult profession in the world. No one is ever secure and no one ever knows when they'll be working again. "You're only as good as your last job" is a very well-known theatrical phrase. So it's an urgent endeavour always to keep going.' But it is most certainly more than that, and he goes on to say, 'I think it's a marvellous profession – if you have a good job it is very rewarding. If you make people laugh, and entertain them, that is very satisfying.'

He clearly loves his work, and wants to continue, because as he says, the work keeps him sharp and focused. He's a bit skeptical about retirement when you do work that you love. He told us about the best part of working:

> You should make sure you find something to do which occupies your brain and makes you think and work creatively. I honestly believe that's one of the reasons I've lived to be the ripe old age that I am. I have used my brain constructively and very forcefully all my life. I'm sure that keeps you going and keeps you younger than your years.

Slightly dismissive of retirement, he says, 'The number of people who have settled jobs then retire at 65 and start puttering about in the garden or things like that – I notice that many of them just fade away when they reach to 70 or 80.'

There are two points to take from this experience. The first is that many people keep working and enjoy the fact that working into later age keeps them sharp, focused and interested. If you enjoy your job and think that the effort and value you put into it are equal to the benefits you get out of it, then why would you want to retire? Skills and experience are only enhanced from continued practice, and sometimes a veteran is more valuable than a novice.

The second point is for employers and managers considering the value of early retirement, retirement at 65 or keeping on workers past 65. This is a simple and clear argument: if people are good at their job, qualified and experienced and want to do the job, there is no valid reason not to work with them. This point has been made throughout this book. Hire, promote and keep the best workers who are the best for the job. If someone is qualified and competent, if they are the best person for they job, it doesn't matter whether they are 18 or 95 – all that matters is their ability to do the job. Select the best people based on their ability and performance.

Individual cases and context

There are all sorts of reasons people believe the retirement age should be 65. From previous legal guidelines to cultural norms to changes in life expectancies, there is a persistent myth that at around 50- or 60-something years old, people start to want or need retirement.

There's also the individual context. Most people have colleagues for whom retirement can't come quickly enough. Some people eagerly await their own retirement, others never want to retire. There are some cases when people should almost certainly retire at 65 or earlier. Joseph Stalin died in office at 74, and perhaps it would have not been a terrible thing if he had taken an earlier retirement.

The main point is that a retirement age may have been a boon for workers when employment rights were limited and people were worked to death with little or no rights to pensions, retirement or social security. That is no longer the case – of course people who enjoy a long and productive working life should have the opportunity to enjoy a retirement. At the same time, retirement is not a bucolic dream for everyone. There are many reasons that people enjoy their work, and for many people, working at older ages does not necessarily mean a 40-hour week or a nine-to-five job.

A retirement age of 65 is obsolete in the modern economy because there are so many different options for working later (as well as earlier) in life. There are flexible working arrangements or job sharing. People can work as consultants in the skills they have mastered over a lifetime. They can do project work or arrange any number of different working arrangements. Why should someone who is experienced, talented, qualified and who wants to work be forced to retire? Furthermore, there is evidence that retirement is not always good for health, wellness or happiness – particularly for people forced to retire when they would rather be working.

Conclusion

Mandatory retirement ages make sense when they are meant to protect workers from being exploited. They make absolutely no sense when they take qualified, intelligent, talented people out of work against their will. It makes no sense for workers who bring a great deal to their work and workplace to leave against their will. It also makes no sense to remove people (who want to be there) from the workplace.

This is consistent with what has been said throughout this book. If people like their work, if they are qualified and will do the best job, there should not be barriers to getting the job based on irrelevant factors like age, gender, ethnicity, sexual orientation or any factor that does not affect their performance.

References and further reading

Centres for Disease Control and Prevention (CDC) (2015) United States Life Tables, 2011, *National Vital Statistics Reports*, 64 (11). Available at: https://www.cdc.gov/nchs/data/nvsr/nvsr64/nvsr64_11.pdf

Halleröd, B, Örestig, J and Stattin, M (2013) Leaving the labour market: the impact of exit routes from employment to retirement on health and wellbeing in old age, *European Journal of Ageing*, 10 (1), pp 23–35

Office for National Statistics (ONS) (2014) Life expectancy at birth and at age 65 by local areas in the United Kingdom: 2006–08 to 2010–12, Office for National Statistics. Available at: https://www.ons.gov.uk/peoplepopulationandcommunity/birthsdeathsandmarriages/lifeexpectancies/bulletins/lifeexpectancyatbirthandatage65bylocalareasintheunitedkingdom/2014-04-16

van der Heide, I et al (2013) Is retirement good for your health? A systematic review of longitudinal studies, *BMC Public Health*, 13 (1180)

Wunsch, C and Raman, J V (2010) Mandatory retirement in the United Kingdom, Canada and the United States of America, *The Age and Employment Network*. Available at: http://www.taen.org.uk/uploads/resources/Combined_dissertation_final_formatted1.pdf

- MYTH 17 -

PERFECTIONISTS MAKE THE BEST EMPLOYEES

Perfectionism can be a blessing or a curse.

Introduction

Perfectionism seems like it should be a good thing: an admirable trait. We often see what looks like perfection and perfectionists in successful athletes, business people, politicians and across social media. The online world often lends itself to carefully selected, curated and tweaked content to try to create a perfect image for individuals or companies.

It can be more challenging to create an image of perfection at work, when daily mistakes or errors are in view of colleagues and bosses. Some people have perfectionistic tendencies whereas others constantly seem to let minor errors slip through.

Wouldn't it be nice to be perfect? Perhaps if it were possible. What about being a perfectionist? Serena Williams, for example, describing herself said, 'I get really angry and I'm a perfectionist.' And of course she is one of the best tennis players in the world, climbing up the ranks in the record books with 23 Grand Slam titles (Mirza, 2017).

It is easy to admire perfectionists when they succeed but is it really such a desirable attribute to have in employees? When it is used and channeled appropriately it can lead to high standards, flawless work and fantastic results. But when it goes wrong (as it often does) it can be a psychological handicap that hinders performance, creates conflict with others, leads to missed deadlines and makes those perfectionists profoundly unhappy. So should we view perfectionists as having a healthy drive to achieve things or on the contrary as having a self-destructive and overdemanding outlook?

The concept of the perfectionist can be both positive and negative. There is the idea of the nit-picker – someone who looks for the hole in a transparent window. But we talk about the perfect holiday, the perfect meal and cry with delight, 'Sheer perfection.' Surely then, those who seek to produce it in the kitchen or factory, studio or office are admirable people worth having as employees?

Problems with perfectionism

Perfectionists prioritize and pursue excellence, striving to meet goals that are important to them or their work. In most workplaces perfectionism is seen as the goal for standard employees, something to be encouraged. The conscientious employee who always wants to do well and produce their best work is certainly a very valuable employee. Not only do they have high standards, they also tend to have higher standards than any of their colleagues or even their boss. They don't usually need to be motivated to do their best because it is a condition they impose on themselves. Combined with ability and stability, perfectionists can, should and do reach exceptionally high levels of performance. So what's the problem?

Notice that one of the main conditions for optimal performance is stability. There is a clear and distinct dark side to perfectionism. At worst, perfectionists believe they should be perfect: no hesitations, deviations or inconsistencies. They become oversensitive to any perceived or real imperfection, failing or weakness. They also tend to believe that other people's affection and approval depends completely on their own perfection. When they do not feel their work is perfect (and they rarely do) then they get anxious, irritable, unhappy or angry.

Perfectionism can be a strength, but it is also a significant vulnerability at work. Even when perfectionists are top performers they still tend to feel a sense of failure. They measure themselves against where they think they should be and often set goals that are unattainable. There are many difficulties that perfectionism can create, and here are three of the major issues that can occur. First, perfectionism can hinder objective measures of performance; second, it tends to lower subjective measures of performance in reducing job satisfaction; and finally, it can hinder group performance by creating interpersonal conflict.

1 Hinders performance

As previously mentioned, perfectionism can be effective in certain situations. But take away the stability, throw in an unexpected challenge – a fight with a colleague, or any minor additional source of stress – and it can push the perfectionist overboard. For many perfectionists, even minor problems can push them over the edge and into counterproductive behaviours and emotions, distracting them from the task at hand.

The perfectionist also has a tendency to be indecisive and is surprisingly likely to miss deadlines. When nothing is ever good enough, how do you know when it is finished? The more time the perfectionist gets, the more time they may take to obsess over details, even details that do not matter. For a perfectionist, anxiety over the quality of their work may overpower the need to get things done on time. They might decide to submit work late or not at all instead of letting other people see work they view as substandard (even if the work is of high quality).

That is not to say this is true of all perfectionists. When stress is managed effectively, with a bit of self-awareness and with trusted colleagues, the perfectionist might perform extremely well.

2 Lowers satisfaction

One issue is concern over mistakes, which reflects negative reactions to mistakes, a tendency to interpret mistakes as equivalent to failure, and a tendency to believe that one will lose the respect of others following failure ('People will probably think less of me if I make a mistake'; 'I should be upset if I make a mistake'). A second issue is of personal standards which reflect the setting of very high standards and the importance placed on these high standards for self-evaluation ('If I do not set the highest standards for myself, I am likely to end up a second-rate person'; 'I hate being less than the best at things'). The tendency to believe that one's parents set very high goals comprises the third issue of parental expectations ('My parents expected excellence from me'; 'My parents wanted me to be the best at everything'). Fourth, the perception that one's parents are (or were) overly critical constitutes the parental criticism ('As a child I was punished for doing things less than perfectly'; 'I never felt like I could meet my parents' standards'). Another feature is the doubting of actions, which reflects the extent to which people doubt their ability to accomplish tasks. Finally, excessive importance can be placed on order and organization ('Organization is very important to me'; 'I try to be a neat person').

Pathological perfectionists are both unhappy and unproductive. They tend to have low self-esteem because they feel they are losers. And there is always the ghost of guilt and its fellow travellers, shame and self-recrimination. Most perfectionists struggle with depression, pessimism and low self-belief. They can easily become immobilized and without motivation. But when they are at it, perfectionists are marked by their compulsivity, obsession and rigidity.

3 Creates interpersonal challenges

Perfectionists measure themselves against their own personal standards. If their standards are unreasonable, there are many ways this can lead to conflict.

Perfectionists typically place a great deal of value on the opinions of others, particularly their line manager or senior leadership. They may set much higher standards for themselves than is reasonable, and then feel like they are letting others down. Whether their perfectionism comes from a desire to do their best or to please other people, their desire to please is often more of a distraction and source of stress than an asset for them at work.

Working for a perfectionist can be an extremely frustrating and demotivating experience. They may never be satisfied with your work, pointing out all your mistakes, no matter how small. They may be an inspiring figure, but often they get frustrated in a leadership or management role when they believe they would be able to do other people's work better themselves. Often they get sidetracked by minutiae and forget the bigger picture.

Conclusion

When you see someone who appears to be perfect, or get frustrated with the perfectionist at work, empathy may be a more appropriate response than envy. They are often driven by fear of making mistakes or disapproval. This can easily lead into a downward cycle of unrealistic goals, failing to reach those goals, becoming anxious or depressed, then being less able to cope with their more realistic goals. This means perfectionists are not necessarily the best employees, as the title of Neville's (2013) *Forbes* article points out: 'Perfectionism is the enemy of everything.'

Perfectionism can be a blessing or a curse. There's nothing wrong with setting high standards, but standards need to be realistic. Perfectionists need help and support just like everyone else. It is okay to be human, but not possible to be superhuman. There's nothing wrong with providing a meaningful contribution to the success of a team, even if it is not the largest contribution.

And those who do create an image of perfection are not practically perfect in every way, no matter how much they measure on one particular aspect of success.

References

Mirza, R (2017) How Serena Williams won a record 23rd Grand Slam titles with victory at the Australian Open, *Sky Sports*, 19 April. Available at: http://www.skysports.com/tennis/news/12110/10742619/how-serena-williams-won-a-record-23rd-grand-slam-titles-with-victory-at-the-australian-open

Neville, A (2013) Perfectionism is the enemy of everything, *Forbes*, 10 May. Available at: https://www.forbes.com/sites/amandaneville/2013/05/10/perfectionism-is-the-enemy-of-everything/#3b5c595b6fd3

- MYTH 18 -

WOMEN AREN'T AS COMPETITIVE AS MEN AT WORK

Just because women's competitiveness can look different from the way men compete, it does not mean women aren't competitive in the workplace.

Introduction

Gender stereotypes would suggest that men are more competitive than their female colleagues. Men are supposedly more aggressive, more dominant and more competitive. Women are apparently more collaborative and cooperative, nurturers and carers instead of chest-thumping aggressors.

The evolutionary psychologists would say that these stereotypes can be explained in the human history of evolution (Puts, 2010). In primitive societies, men were hunters and fighters and women were gatherers and nurturers; these roles have been hardwired over evolutionary history so as to be natural in modern society. Of course, extending these ideas to the modern workplace is tenuous at best, and not particularly useful when the evidence from the workplace suggests there's a better way to look at competitiveness at work.

This is interesting and important because competition is not always valuable or useful in every workplace or every type of job (MacRae and Furnham, 2014). There are many types of work that benefit from employees who are less competitive, less demanding of the spotlight and have less need to be seen as the 'winner'.

Women are not all the same

The first, obvious, point is that some women are more competitive than others. The High Potential Trait Inventory (MacRae and Furnham, 2014), which measures competitiveness in the workplace, shows that women are distributed across the continuum of competitiveness, and Teodorescu, Furnham and MacRae (2017) also found women are distributed across the spectrum of competitiveness as much as men in the workplace.

At the most basic level, the evidence doesn't support the claim that women are not as inherently competitive as men in the workplace, but the evidence may indicate that men and women have different styles and ways of being competitive.

Women tend to compete more against other women

Some would suggest (Gordon, 2015) that women tend to be more competitive amongst other women, instead of competing directly with men. Yet Gordon suggests women compete with each other in less direct and confrontational ways and cites a literature review by Vaillancourt (2013) which explains that this female aggression is often channeled into improving their own image while undermining that of their rivals.

There are many competition theories on why women compete with each other. The first is the previously mentioned evolutionary psychology approach that suggests women are essentially using mating strategies that have been evolved over a long period of time to protect themselves physically and thus use indirect instead of direct and physical confrontation methods – while making themselves more attractive than other women. The second theory is that the social value of work, money, prestige and success create aggression in competition for resources.

We're going to leave much of the theory aside for the rest of this discussion, because it is controversial, often overly simplistic, patronizing or ignores the real and practical questions of how competition actually exists in the workplace.

Women prefer to compete against themselves

Apicella, Demiral and Mollerstrom (2017) were interested in gender differences in competitiveness, particularly in relation to how competitiveness affected pay and promotions in the workplace for men and women.

They conducted an experiment where participants were asked to compete in solving simple maths problems either against another hypothetical person or against their own performance. That's similar to beating one's own personal best weekly sales, compared with having higher weekly sales than a colleague.

In round one of the study, participants were paid $1 for every correct question they answered (real financial rewards typically yield results more accurate to how people behave in the workplace, particularly in situations where they are paid for performance). Then, in round two, participants were either asked to beat their own previous scores or those of a randomly assigned opponent. Participants who solved more maths problems than their competition (either their own score or those of a randomly assigned partner) were paid an additional $2 for every correctly solved problem. Participants who solved fewer problems received nothing in this round.

To boost the competitiveness factor, participants were given a choice in round three. They could choose either to be paid the lower amount ($1) for every problem solved correctly in a non-competitive task, or they could choose to be paid the higher amount ($2) with the more competitive rules. This stage was where the major gender differences appeared.

Apicella and colleagues found that in the 'other' condition, men were significantly more likely to choose to compete against another person for the higher reward and women were more likely to choose the lower-value reward under the non-competitive circumstances. However, in the 'self' condition, women were just as likely to choose to compete with their own past performance as men for the higher reward. This is an important distinction, showing that even though some women appear to be less competitive with colleagues, they can be just as competitive about improving and maximizing their own performance. Just because women's competitiveness can look different from the way men compete, it does not mean women aren't competitive in the workplace.

Financial and workplace implications

Lower competitiveness is often offered as an explanation of why women get paid less than their male counterparts in the workplace (Apicella and Mollerstrom, 2017). Indeed, competitiveness may help individuals stand out, display their performance and get attention for it in the workplace. In competitive workplace cultures, it may be easiest to stand out as a high performer by showing that one's performance is better than those of colleagues.

However, competing with others, especially others within the company, can be counterproductive. A bit of healthy competition can be useful, but when it gets out of hand, competitiveness can lead to aggressive and ultimately destructive behaviours like malicious gossip, bullying, sabotaging colleagues' performance and infighting. An excessively competitive culture can be counterproductive when time is spent bringing others' performance down to elevate oneself. Ultimately, it is not ideal to be the top performer in a race to the bottom.

That being said, competitiveness is not inherently toxic or dangerous – used constructively it can be an excellent motivator. Competitiveness is often used as a motivation tool in the world of work, whether it is competitiveness between salespeople, athletes or competing companies. The interesting point raised by Apicella and Mollerstrom (2017) from their research findings is that people who compete with themselves improve their performance the same amount as those who compete with others. Competition can help to boost performance, but the nature and type of that competition can take many forms.

Conclusion

Women can be as competitive as men in the workplace, but not everyone is competitive, irrespective of their gender. Women tend to compete more with their own personal best than with their colleagues. Performance evaluations must measure improvements of individual performance as well as performance in relation to colleagues.

References

Apicella, C and Mollerstrom, J (2017) Women do like to compete – against themselves, *New York Times*, 24 February. Available at: https://www.nytimes.com/2017/02/24/opinion/sunday/women-do-like-to-compete-against-themselves.html

Apicella, C, Demiral, E E and Mollerstrom, J (2017) *No Gender Differences in Willingness to Compete when Competing against Self*, DIW Berlin Discussion Paper No 1638

Gordon, E V (2015) Why women compete with each other, *New York Times*, 31 October. Available at: https://www.nytimes.com/2015/11/01/opinion/sunday/why-women-compete-with-each-other.html?mtrref=www.google.ca&gwh=9A27BDAC3F5A01FEB9E44DBE6E44116B&gwt=pay&assetType=opinion

MacRae, I and Furnham, A (2014) *High Potential: How to spot, manage and develop talented people at work*, Bloomsbury, London

Puts, D A (2010) Beauty and the beast: mechanisms of sexual selection in humans, *Evolution & Human Behavior*, **31** (3), pp 157–75

Teodorescu, A, Furnham, A and MacRae, I (2017) Trait correlates of success at work, *International Journal of Selection and Assessment*, **25**, pp 36–42

Vaillancourt, T (2013) Do human females use indirect aggression as an intrasexual competition strategy? *Philosophical Transactions of the Royal Society B*, **368** (1631)

- MYTH 19 -

PEOPLE'S PERSONALITIES CAN BE SORTED INTO CATEGORIES AT WORK

Understanding your own personality traits and those of your colleagues means understanding their tendencies and how they are likely to approach the work. There are no 'wrong' personality trait levels because each has unique strengths and weaknesses.

Introduction

Robert Benchley (1920) amusingly noticed that 'There may be said to be two classes of people in the world: those who constantly divide the people of the world into two classes and those who do not. Both classes are extremely unpleasant to meet socially, leaving practically no one in the world whom one cares very much to know.' This is often done for personality traits – people are divided into one category or another. People are either conscientious or not. There are the curious and the traditionalists. Then there are the people who are cooperative or competitive. Some people are thinkers, other are doers. Then Category X will clash with Category Z.

Supposedly, the 'opposite' types don't like, understand or respect each other. Can personalities really be that different that people will automatically clash? And can we reduce people into two personality categories?

The concept of personality clash does not come from the terminology of psychology and psychiatry. Still, psychologists, consultants and trainers are often eager to jump on the bandwagon. In these circumstances, there are nearly always personality traits which are defined as two opposing types: ideal for the clash. People with different personality traits may be more likely to clash, but it is essential to use valid models of personality to assess this (MacRae and Furnham, 2014).

The term 'personality clash' typically is used when people have a disagreement because of their different personality traits, values, work ethic or other attributes. People can thus have very different ways of thinking and behaving at work. It's not just dislike or distrust; personality clash can reflect differences in the way people see the world. It can be very challenging to work with colleagues who seem fundamentally different. Early risers or morning types loathe meetings at four o'clock in the afternoon and can't believe night owls actually do work after 5:30, while the latter are never sure, but can't confirm, precisely when the morning larks arrive at the office or what, if anything, they do then.

Personality clashes can occur at very different levels of severity, and levels of severity can be a more helpful way of thinking about personality clash than a categorical method. There are various popular models of personality in the workplace, such as the Myers-Briggs Type Indicators, which sort people into different categories. They are either introverts who prefer time on their own, or gregarious extroverts who get energy from being around other people. Many people believe that people can easily be sorted into personality categories at work, but the scientific evidence would indicate otherwise. Sorting people into A/B categories is not the most effective way of understanding personality at work (MacRae and Furnham, 2014). To explore and understand this it is useful to talk about trait and type models of personality.

Trait vs type clashes

The two major categories of personality theory can be divided between trait- and type-based models.

1 Type models are categorical: they sort people into groups based on one or more personality variables. For example, *Type A* personality is a term often used to describe a high-strung, driven and competitive personality type; *Type B* personalities are said to be more relaxed, less driven and less competitive. In other instances, multiple personality variables are used and may be described as categories, colours, acronyms or various other identifiers.

2 Trait models describe people based on a level, or score, of a particular pattern of thoughts and behaviour. In trait models, an individual's personality can be described as a location on the continuum of stable factors. Different locations on a particular trait continuum describe absence or presence of the same and similar thoughts and behaviour. For example, curiosity describes an approach to new information and novelty which can be like, dislike, ambivalence or anywhere in between.

Traits are a much more accurate and nuanced way to explain personality traits, and can be most informative about personality clash. Personality trait scores manifest in a normal distribution.

A type model of personality would only be a valid and useful way of describing personality if distinct 'clusters' of types emerged (which they do not). In the research, personality traits clearly emerge in a normal distribution, where most scores cluster in the centre of the distribution (MacRae and Furnham, 2014). The majority of people cluster in the 'middle', while fewer and fewer have 'extreme' personality traits. Those in the middle of the spectrum tend to be much more similar than people on opposite ends of the spectrum. This is true of nearly all traits, from height to intelligence. Based on these findings and trends, the most valid method of describing personality is using a trait-based model. It is also the most informative and nuanced way to look at personality clashes.

Personality traits and how they clash

The High Potential Traits Inventory (MacRae and Furnham, 2014; Teodorescu, Furnham and MacRae, 2017) measures six personality traits in the workplace. These traits can be used to explain where common personality clashes happen at work.

Conscientiousness

Conscientiousness is a combination of self-discipline, organization and impulse control. Individuals who have high conscientiousness tend to be well organized and prefer to make concrete plans. They are very good at motivating themselves, they appear driven and like to accomplish goals. Individuals with lower conscientiousness are more casual about deadlines and timeframes. They appear to 'go with the flow' and may gain more satisfaction from things unrelated to career goals, achievements or accolades.

Higher conscientiousness has similar effects on group performance as on individual performance. Furthermore, every team or group benefits from at least one person with high conscientiousness who can motivate the team and is able to set clear goals and timeframes. However, teams full of people with only high conscientiousness can sometimes be particularly inward-focused and rule-bound.

People at the high and low ends of the conscientiousness spectrum can clash when they appear to have very different work ethics and diligence. Those with low conscientiousness may view higher-conscientiousness workers as rigid, obsessive-compulsive perfectionists. In reverse, those with high conscientiousness may see lower-conscientiousness colleagues as lazy or unfocused.

People with higher conscientiousness are better in detail-oriented tasks that require long-term planning and self-motivation. Those with lower conscientiousness tend to be better at spontaneous work and environments where they are motivated by their environment, colleagues, events or managers.

Adjustment

Adjustment describes how individuals react emotionally to stressors, circumstances and relationships with other individuals. People with low adjustment think more negative thoughts and become preoccupied with negative emotions. People who have lower adjustment are more likely to be self-conscious about their work, their actions and how they behave around others. Low adjustment is associated with negative thoughts, concern and unnecessary embarrassment. Adjustment is related to generally feeling more positive about one's own work, performance and relationships. Those with higher adjustment become less preoccupied with demands and strains, and are more confident about their performance.

Adjustment has a great impact on how people interact and work with others. Individuals with lower adjustment can become preoccupied with the opinions of others, and may spend excessive amounts of time ruminating about minor interactions. Individuals with higher adjustment consider situations, but are much less likely to be unnecessarily self-conscious or embarrassed. Lower-adjustment workers can be seen as neurotic, while those with the highest adjustment may seem cold or uncaring.

Those with higher adjustment are better at dealing with stressful situations, tasks and jobs. They do well in work where they need to be calm and collected under fire. Those with lower adjustment can be effective in work environments where they need to be sensitive to external threats or risks.

Curiosity

Curiosity describes a person's approach to new information, methods and approaches. Those who are curious actively search for new information and alternative methods of getting work done. Curious individuals actively seek out new information. Those with lower curiosity levels prefer tried-and-tested approaches, can be suspicious of new information and dislike experimenting with new techniques.

Individuals with high curiosity are interested in others' opinions and ways of working. They like to ask questions and understand how and why other people are working in certain ways. People with higher curiosity may need more information to be engaged, whereas individuals with lower curiosity may be less interested in discussion and in understanding others' motivations.

Those with high curiosity can be perceived as unfocused and may have a tendency to jump from idea to idea or project or project. Those on the low end of the spectrum may be seen as more traditional, conventional and may seem to block innovation or progress.

Employees with higher curiosity tend to succeed in positions that require learning new information and ways of doing things. They also tend to learn faster from training and development programmes. Those with lower curiosity are better with tasks and jobs that require strong, stable and consistently reliable performers.

Risk approach

Risk approach is how a person deals with challenging, difficult or threatening situations. Those with high risk approach consider a broad range of options, choose what they believe to be the best and then act quickly. Conversely, those with a lower risk approach tend to react to circumstances. Those who have high risk approach are willing to confront challenges directly and immediately. Individuals with lower risk approach tend to avoid challenges or conflict until they have no other choice.

Risk approach is a predictor of how people interact with other group members. Those high in 'courage' are good at being assertive and confronting problems, but may sometimes appear to be overly aggressive. Those who are more reactive avoid conflict and risk.

Most groups benefit from individuals with a range of risk approach traits. Groups benefit from individuals who are able to confront risk, but groups with many courageous individuals can become fractious or antagonistic. Groups without courageous members can be overly risk averse and may be unable to resolve inter-group conflict.

Different levels of risk approach often lead to personality clashes when those who avoid conflict at any cost come up against those who like to take a direct and forward approach to conflict or difficult situations. Those with lower risk approach may be more effective in roles that do not involve a great deal of interpersonal conflict or work risks.

Ambiguity acceptance

Ambiguity acceptance describes reaction to mixed information and complexity. Individuals with high ambiguity acceptance enjoy complex situations and uncertainty. Individuals with low ambiguity acceptance find divergent information and uncertainty difficult or frustrating and prefer straightforward problems, situations and solutions.

Ambiguity acceptance can be a characteristic of businesses and organizations, as well as individuals. An organization with flexible policies and high tolerance for individual decision making demonstrates high ambiguity acceptance. Other organizations have clearly documented and rigid hierarchies, business processes and guidelines that suggest low ambiguity tolerance.

Ambiguity acceptance affects how individuals interact with others at work. Those with high ambiguity acceptance enjoy complex and diverse information. They are more likely to seek out conflicting opinions, or evidence that contradicts their current understanding. Individuals with low ambiguity acceptance dislike mixed messages and get frustrated when they feel people aren't being clear. They are more likely to avoid conflicting opinions, which can lead to leadership derailment.

Workers with different levels of ambiguity acceptance come into conflict when those with high ambiguity acceptance seem vague or send mixed messages and those on the lower end of the spectrum want clarity and certainty. Those with higher ambiguity acceptance tend to be better in strategic leadership roles. Employees with low ambiguity acceptance are often more successful in technical or specialist roles.

Competitiveness

Competitiveness represents a person's desire to win, their need for power and their reaction to winning or losing. Individuals with higher competitiveness need to feel that their achievements are recognized and appreciated. Higher competitiveness can drive performance and improvement. Individuals with lower competitiveness feel less need for control and are less focused on receiving awards or recognition.

Competitiveness affects how individuals perform in groups and how they interact with the rest of the team. Individuals who are very competitive see team events as an opportunity to demonstrate their ability. They also desire recognition from other team members for their achievements. People with lower competitiveness can be equally effective in teams, but may not want to stand out and may gain more satisfaction from the team's overall success than their own achievement.

Clearly clashes will occur when the competitive worker wants to compete with those who dislike competition. Those with high competitiveness may always want to be seen as the 'winner', while their colleagues who are lower on the spectrum do not want to compete or be in the spotlight.

Those high in competitiveness often succeed in roles that demand high individual performance and competition with others. Sales people and elite athletes tend to benefit from high competitiveness. Those with lower competitiveness are better in jobs where they need to be collaborative team players.

Meeting in the middle

While people on opposite ends of the spectrum tend to be the most different and most likely to have personality clashes, those in the middle tend to be most similar, and less likely to clash.

This is important, because understanding your own personality traits and those of your colleagues means understanding their tendencies and how they are likely to approach the work. There are no 'wrong' personality trait levels because each has unique strengths and weaknesses. Some jobs fit different personality profiles better than others, so employers should work to fit employees with positions and tasks that fit the strengths of the individual. How to do this is discussed in great detail in *High Potential: How to spot, manage and develop talented people at work* (MacRae and Furnham, 2014).

Conclusion

Different personalities can and do clash in the workplace, and the best way to predict and prevent clashes, or mitigate their negative effects is to understand the different personality traits. It is helpful to remember that personality traits are enduring patterns of thought, emotion and behaviour. It is very unlikely that personalities will change, so understanding the effects they can have on work and how people interact is the best route to minimizing clashes. Although, inevitably, personality clashes will certainly still happen at work, understanding how personality traits fit with different types of work will help to minimize conflict and maximize performance.

References and further reading

Benchley, R (1920) The most popular book of the month: an extremely literary review of the latest edition of the New York City Telephone Directory, *Vanity Fair*, February 1920

Caspi, A, Roberts, B W and Shiner, R L (2005) Personality development: stability and change, *Annual Review of Psychology*, 56, pp 453–84

MacRae, I and Furnham, A (2014) *High Potential: How to spot, manage and develop talented people at work*, Bloomsbury, London

McCrae, R R et al (2000) Nature over nurture: temperament, personality, and life span development, *Journal of Personality and Social Psychology*, 78 (1), p 173

Teodorescu, A, Furnham, A and MacRae, I (2017) Trait correlates of success at work, *International Journal of Selection and Assessment*, 25, pp 35–40

– MYTH 20 –

SEXUALITY AND GENDER SHOULD BE TAKEN INTO ACCOUNT AT WORK

Equity is not about giving anyone a job, nor is it about an artificial quota system, but it is about making sure people who are capable and qualified for the job have equal opportunities to succeed.

Introduction

Ian Fleming, author of the James Bond novels, was a fantastic writer of enjoyable books, but had some crazy old ideas. One of these ideas made its way into *The Man with the Golden Gun*: 'There is a popular theory that a man who cannot whistle has homosexual tendencies' (Fleming, 1965).

This is one of the more amusing myths about homosexuality that is both easy to disprove and slightly strange. It does nicely illustrate that there are a host of myths about people with different sexual orientations that may be odd and often irrelevant to the workplace.

This can be one of the more challenging topics, because there are a range of controversies, beliefs and attitudes on the topic on all sides of the ideological and political spectrums. This is beyond the scope of this chapter. There are also some delicacies surrounding terminology that we will briefly mention and largely sidestep in the next section. But before moving on, it will be helpful to summarize the key message of this chapter.

Sexuality and gender identities bring with them many myths and preconceptions within the workplace. There are sometimes biases against people with different sexual orientations at work but these should not be taken as relevant to a person's potential performance.

A note about terminology

A discussion of the range of sexualities and genders is far beyond the scope of this chapter, but for anyone interested in the detailed discussion, we recommended reading Badgett et al (2013). The term to be used in the rest of this chapter will be LGBT+, which is an acronym that stands for Lesbian, Gay, Bisexual and Transgender, plus the many other groups of sexual and gender minorities. There are a variety of different acronyms that can be used to represent different groups, but the main thing to remember for the purpose of this chapter is not to get too hung up on the terminology.

Before venturing further into the more detailed issues, the most important thing to remember is that the point of this chapter is that sexuality and gender are essentially irrelevant when considering selection, development and retention decisions at work. Employees and employers alike benefit from widening the employee talent pool and removing barriers to employment that have nothing to do with predicting actual performance.

The employment equity argument

The argument about hiring, promoting, developing and working with LGBT+ people is the same as for working with or hiring anyone. MacRae and Furnham (2014) describe how employment equity relates to fair practice and good business. Many individuals and companies worry about issues such as these, afraid they be will open to legal challenges or accusations of discrimination. Many companies worry about saying the wrong thing or making the wrong decision and causing a storm on social media. That is why the argument for employment equity will be made entirely in a business case in this chapter.

There is a clear and straightforward argument that employment equity provides a competitive business advantage. If there really is a war for talent or talent shortages then it would be ludicrous for employers to exclude certain people from the workforce if they are qualified and talented. The point of employment equity is that it just means making sure people are judged based on their talent or potential to do the work, and irrelevant factors are ignored.

Employment equity is closely tied to the concepts of talent and potential. Employment equity is about reducing barriers to employment which prevent individuals or groups of people from getting jobs or promotions where they have the potential to succeed. Equity is not about giving *anyone* a job, nor is it about an artificial quota system, but it is about making sure people who are capable and qualified for the job have equal opportunities to succeed. In other words, equity is about identifying potential and performance based on evidence and valid criteria about what makes people actually successful. Singling out and removing people based on specific but irrelevant criteria is not just unfair, it's bad for business.

As described in *High Potential: How to spot, manage and develop talented people at work* (MacRae and Furnham, 2014), there are five main points to be made for employment equity, four of which are included here, which consider LGBT+ people as well as all workers:

1 **It's the right decision.** Employment equity is the right option in terms of morality, validity and being the right business decision. There is no good reason in business to unfairly exclude people for reasons that do not affect their performance or capacity to do the job.

2 **It's a good legal decision.** The legality on the topic essentially says that there are legal problems with unfairly discriminating against any group. That is not to say that businesses must hire people based on attributes like sexuality or gender, but it is unfair and unlawful to make hiring and firing decisions on characteristics that are not relevant to performance. This is typically referred to as a *bona fide occupational qualification (BFOQ)*. It really just means that legally, people should be hired using qualifications that are relevant to the work. For example, firefighters need to have certain physical fitness requirements (UK Fire Services, 2011). These requirements are essential for doing the job well, for example being able to carry equipment or climb a ladder. These are necessary characteristics

to complete the job, but are genuine and legitimate qualifications irrespective of other considerations.

Equitable HR practice brings additional benefit when employees perceive their workplace as being fair, equitable and based on relevant attributes. When employees see their workplaces or its HR practices as unfair, the organization is more likely to lose talent through higher employee turnover (Kerr-Phillips and Thomas, 2009). Workplaces which are perceived to be equitable, with fair and transparent criteria for hiring, promoting and firing tend to be perceived as more desirable places to work.

3 **It increases efficiency and broadens the talent pool.** A major business argument for employment equity is that it broadens the talent pool, reducing the likelihood that talented people will be missed based on irrelevant criteria. When biases against LGBT+ people or any other group are introduced into work, the number of potential employees who will be hired, trained or promoted is reduced. Other companies which do not discriminate against certain groups of people will have a competitive advantage and more potential talent to draw from.

4 **It increases learning and breadth of knowledge.** A more open, intelligent and valid employment policy leads to a more diverse range of talented people at work. Most companies have a fairly broad range of groups as customers, clients or employees. A broader range of life experience, understanding and range of perspectives is a competitive business advantage. It gives the teams in the organization a broader base of people and colleagues to learn from. One of the most obvious examples is that of marketing. Often, homogenous teams end up producing some trite or irrelevant advertisement targeted at a certain group that ends up appearing more alienating or ignorant than insightful. Different perspectives can mitigate or improve this.

Conclusion

The point has been made in many different forms that abandoning silly stereotypes, myths about gays not being able to whistle or other forms of discrimination is good for business. Angel Gurría, secretary general of the Organization for Economic Cooperation and Development, makes a very strong argument that employment equity and removing discrimination from the workforce will actually fuel economic and business growth (Gurría, 2012). Former US ambassador to the OECD, Karen Kornbluh, called this the 'leaky pipeline' of skills, making the point that the more people who are ignored, not hired or not recognized for the skills and knowledge they bring to work, the more the detriment to business and economies (USCIB, 2012).

References

Badgett, M V L et al (2013) The business impact of LGBT-supportive workplace policies, Williams Institute. Available at: https://williamsinstitute.law.ucla.edu/ wp-content/uploads/Business-Impact-of-LGBT-Policies-May-2013.pdf

Fleming, I (1965/2012) *The Man with the Golden Gun: James Bond 007*, Vintage Classics, London

Gurría, A (2012) *All on Board for Gender Equality*, Speech presented at the launch of gender reports, OECD. Available at: http://www.oecd.org/about/secretary-general/allonboardforgenderequality.htm

Kerr-Phillips, B and Thomas, A (2009) Macro and micro challenges for talent retention in South Africa, *South African Journal of Human Resource Management*, 7 (1)

MacRae, I and Furnham, A (2014) *High Potential: How to spot, manage and develop talented people at work*, Bloomsbury, London

UK Fire Services (2011) The Physical Tests: UK Fire Service Resources. Available at: http://www.fireservice.co.uk/recruitment/physical

USCIB (2012) New report on women's economic empowerment launched at OECD ministerial. Available at: http://www.uscib.org/new-report-on-womens-economic-empowerment-launched-at-oecd-ministerial-ud-4330/

- MYTH 21 -

MILLENNIALS ARE CHANGING THE WORKPLACE

Generational differences are no more helpful to understanding employees than the date they were born.

Introduction

There is a persistent and pernicious myth that different generations are fundamentally different in factors like personality, values and the way they work. The myth that there are fundamental or inherent differences between generations can have a great deal of impact on the way people are hired, promoted, managed and retained in the workplace (MacRae and Furnham, 2017). However, there is limited evidence to support the idea that there are major generational differences, and a great deal of evidence to show there are more important factors to consider in the workplace.

There is extensive interest regarding generational differences in popular writing, media and business publications. Much (but not all) of the commentary about younger people or 'Millennials' tends to be quite negative. Generally, the generations are thought to be separable by factors like their attitudes and values, and shaped by the events of the particular time they grow up in. Growing up at a particular time and place and in certain circumstances often leaves a very strong mark on people. Societies, communities, families and schools all try to teach their members a certain set of beliefs and values about important issues and appropriate types of behaviour. They instil judgements and attitudes about what is right or wrong, good or bad, just or unjust, fair or unfair.

The ideas about generational differences take this further and assume everyone born within a certain time period of about 25 years has shared experiences, values and traits. This is a typical stereotyping of someone in a different age group by another generational category. The other generation is viewed as fundamentally different, with everyone in that age category being all the same. All the while it's much easier to see the wide degree of variation in values, motivation, personality and career attainment within one's own age group.

Generational differences are an oversimplification that reduces people into overly simplistic 'us' vs 'them' categories. First, we're going to explain why it is so clearly a myth, then explain why there is much to learn from debunking this myth.

The root of the myth

The question about generational differences is often raised, imagining generations are like different tribes or different cultures with a magical cut-off point to distinguish between them. Everyone born between 1943 and 1960 is similar. Sorry 1961, you're out and stuck with the 1981-ers.

First, we'll discuss the purported generational differences, and the supposed attributes of common generational categories. If generational differences in work values and attitudes do exist, it should be straightforward to define the generations and measure any differences that do exist in the workplace. Logically, then, if generations are different, it would follow that they need to be managed differently and need different working conditions.

The most widespread theory of generational differences is the Strauss-Howe model. Their generational terminology has become widespread. The

Baby Boomers were born around 1943–1960 and were shaped by the aftermath of World War II. Generation X was born between 1961 and 1981 and the Millennials between 1982 and 2004 (this means that technically 'Millennials' are now between 13 and 35 years old). The next generation entering the workforce now are technically the 'Homeland Generation', who, according to Strauss-Howe, would have similar characteristics to the 'Greatest Generation', born between 1925 and 1942 – the generation which fought in World War II.

The *Baby Boomers,* who were born after World War II, have been shaped by the turbulent '60s when they challenged the assumptions and what they perceived to be injustice going on in the world. This is the generation of civil rights, Woodstock, the moon landings, sit-ins, hijackings and nuclear power. The Baby Boomers are supposed to dislike traditional hierarchies and act out against conformity. They are happy to experiment with new things.

Generation X-ers have been influenced by the events of the '70s and '80s. They lived through one of the worst economic depressions since the Great Depression of the 1930s. They grew up with environmental movements, the women's movement, the decline of manufacturing and the rise of the service industry. They tend to get a bad reputation at work, appearing disloyal to anyone who was loyal to them. They were told 'greed is good', and were lampooned for their selfish 'yuppie' culture of materialism and self-indulgence.

Millennials started joining the world of work around the year 2000. They have been supposedly shaped by the '90s: the end of the USSR, the unification of Germany, increasing unification of Europe, the end of apartheid and a more interconnected, interdependent world of globalization. Their world started to shrink rapidly with the rise of information technology. Machines and technology started to replace people at work at an even more rapid pace and people became nomadic, working from home, sharing desks, and relying on more unstable or flexible working arrangements.

We read that the new generation entering the workforce – not even Millennials anymore – is changing the workplace. That this new generation is somehow fundamentally different. That emojis and selfies are changing the world more than any previous generation.

The reality is that every generation has faced different challenges. There is nothing new or surprising in the fact that the world and the world of work is changing. It has been changing since the invention of cotton, gin and the printing press, and even before that.

Debunking the myth

If generations are fundamentally different then they will have different expectations of work. For that to be true, general social trends and world events would have to have a more powerful influence on how children develop than their direct environment. And it should be apparent that having a good or bad parent is going to shape a child more than whether or not US–Russia relations are frosty or amicable. A child's peer group has more influence than the current NATO security council. Someone's school and quality of education have more effect on their development as a person than UN resolutions.

There may be common memories people of certain generations share of world events. That's why people grow up and end up having different values, different political beliefs and different ideas about work. People of certain generations may all remember Winston Churchill, Margaret Thatcher or Tony Blair – but people within the same generation do not automatically have the same views about them.

The 'theory' would suggest that major (national and international) cultural, historical and social events have a direct impact on a person's attitudes, beliefs and values. This would mean that whether you grew up in northern England, northern Canada or North Korea during the same time period (historic period), you have a lot in common.

There are at least three significant reasons the generational difference myth can be misleading (a greater discussion of this, and a longer list of reasons, can be found in MacRae and Furnham, 2017):

1 **Ageing.** Quite simply, ageing changes people. People change, learn and develop over time. People, on the whole, tend to get more experience, become more disciplined, and more interpersonally astute over time. Some young people already seem to have 'grown up', some will grow up and some just never seem to. A better explanation is that younger people can be more impulsive and take some time to settle into a working environment. People have blamed the younger generation for being rude, disrespectful, impulsive challengers of authority for centuries and across cultures – from Socrates to Dostoyevsky (MacRae and Furnham, 2014; 2017). This is not a generational phenomenon; most young people develop and mature into working life.

2 **Social experience.** The generational difference myth assumes that social experience is the most important factor. The truth is, there is an

overwhelming amount of evidence to show that intelligence, personality, training, experience and other factors are much better predictors of performance than age or generation. In a job interview, take a dozen random people, all of the same age, and their performance will vary greatly. There may be some young people who are entitled, narcissistic, social media-obsessed show-offs with poor impulse control. But there are people in every generational group that fit that description.

3 **Arbitrary cut-off points.** Categorizing generational differences means arbitrary decisions have to be made to sort people based on date of birth. There tends to be little or no evidence to back up these dates; they are just a general cluster of historical events. It is illogical to classify people by age range the same way a historian would use the dates a monarch reigned to describe a historical period. Two people born within a year (or even one day) of each other are then said to be different, and automatically more similar to someone born 20 years later.

There are plenty of popular books on 'the generations'. Many could be entertaining or enjoyable reading, some confirm people's preconceptions and prejudices, and many are faddish. Generational differences are no more helpful to understanding employees than the date they were born.

There is quite clearly a Generation at Work industry that has built up to profit from the fad. Media articles, TV shows, books and seminars, practitioners and consultants are now all generationists. Everything can be explained by generational membership, and it's one of the new magic bullets that is repackaged and sold.

So what do we know about the evidence to back up the generational differences theory? There is not very much. The theory is weak and illogical. And there's no good reason to suggest it's not just that people change with age.

Over-generalizations and organizational platitudes

The truth is, organizations are changing. The way people work is changing. It always has been, and probably always will be. Much of what is written about generational differences is general HR advice, repackaged and rebranded with 'Millennials' added as a buzzword to flog the books. Business tips like, 'Explain the company vision', 'Provide training and professional development', and 'Clearly communicate job expectations' are good advice for all workers, not just Millennials. Should anyone over a certain age not be told what their job is, not know the company vision and not be given professional development?

Business-savvy marketers of all brands know that it's easy to repackage generic advice and then target it at a specific group. Adding a group like Millennials or older workers or women is a common technique.

Conclusion

Unlike some of the myths in this book which have more equivocal conclusions, there is no evidence to support the myth of generational differences in the workplace. The myth is unhelpful and can even be damaging. At best, it is a few puff pieces and popular books that have no effect. At worst, it is toxic because it is incorrect, misleading and leads to poor, misinformed decision making in the workplace. There are no significant generational differences in the workplace and there are far better factors to measure people on, such as personality, intelligence, individual motivation, skills and experience.

References and further reading

Costanza, D P et al (2012) Generational differences in work-related variables: a meta-analysis, *Journal of Business Psychology*, 27, pp 375–94

MacRae I and Furnham, A (2014) *High Potential: How to spot, manage and develop talented people at work*, Bloomsbury, London

MacRae, I and Furnham, A (2017) *Motivation and Performance: A guide to motivating a diverse workforce*, Kogan Page, London

Senior, J (2017) Having trouble having it all? Ivanka alone can fix it, *New York Times*, 2 May. Available at: https://www.nytimes.com/2017/05/02/books/review-ivanka-trump-women-who-work.html?mtrref=www.google.ca&gwh=00412C8 0D34A51CA3AC2E2940BCED2DF&gwt=pay

Trump, I (2017) *Women Who Work: Rewriting the rules for success*, Portfolio, Uxbridge

– MYTH 22 –

CO-WORKERS SHOULD NOT FORM ROMANTIC RELATIONSHIPS

When lots of people with shared values are pulled into close quarters with a common purpose it should be unsurprising that romantic attractions arise.

Introduction

Is it appropriate for co-workers to form romantic relationships? Ask Bill Clinton or John Major and they might say the consequences of inappropriate trysts can be severe. However, an American study from Stanford University found that about 20 per cent of people met their spouses at work. Indeed, work was the third most common way in which to find a match, exceeded only by meeting through friends and meeting at a bar, club or restaurant (Rosenfeld and Thomas, 2012).

Of course, there are potential problems, and as researchers Pierce and Aguinis (1997) rather unromantically point out, workplace relationships share a key feature with a very undesirable behaviour: 'Workplace romances and sexual harassment share an important characteristic – they both entail a sexual component between two employees.' It should not need a great deal of discussion to say that this chapter is not dealing with the subject of sexual harassment. When we discuss the appropriateness of 'romantic relationships', these are entirely consensual relationships that do not involve abuses of power or position.

It is a difficult topic because, as previously mentioned, about 20 per cent of people meet their spouses at work (which implies that there are likely to be even more workplace relationships than this, as not all will necessarily end in marriage). Most people spend a significant part of their lives at work and it is a way in which many people make lifelong friends and, inevitably, amorous bonds.

Banning romantic office relationships is the tempting and oft-used approach. Perhaps the astronomy department is not allowed to probe any foreign bodies. The marketing department is strictly forbidden from laying out any creative synergies. Heart surgeons who work together are, under no circumstances, to examine any of the nurses, even if they are suffering from acute angina.

Outright bans are unlikely to prevent romances, and may have the opposite effect by making dalliances forbidden, naughty and all that much more exciting. A more nuanced approach is required, along with an understanding that not all types of office relationships are made equal – or inequitable. We discuss some concerns later in the chapter, but first, are there benefits to having office romances?

Perks of office romances

Although the consequences of office romances gone wrong are obvious (spurned lovers, bitter disputes, sexual harassment complaints, exploitation and misuse of power to name a few), there are some perks to falling in love – or lust – at work. Pierce and Aguinas (2003) found that those engaged in office romances had higher levels of job satisfaction and commitment to the organization. This is consistent with findings that, in general, better relations with colleagues improve work satisfaction and performance (Ariani, Ebrahimi and Saeedi, 2011). Other studies indicate that more open, less restrictive policies toward company romance make employees perceive their workplace as a more open, fun and fair place to work (Pierce, Karl and Brey, 2012).

Ariani and colleagues (2011) suggest that contrary to popular belief about workplace romances, most are initiated with good intentions and sincere long-term romantic objectives. Although some office romances begin with casual, insincere or 'utilitarian' (see: carnal) intentions, they suggest these are in the minority. They suggest that participating in a 'satisfactory' office romance can boost job satisfaction and productivity – although one is left a bit unsatisfied at the lengths they go to in defining precisely what constitutes 'satisfaction'.

Power imbalances

Power imbalance can be one of the most pernicious factors in office romances. It's why physicians are not allowed to sleep with their patients or counsellors with their clients. These rules are codified not just in company policy but in professional ethics guidelines.

Romances between colleagues at an equal level on the corporate ladder are a very different beast than co-workers at different places on corporate hierarchies. When colleagues are in the position to trade power, influence, or engage in corporate misbehaviour on behalf of their paramour, the potential risks and consequences are greatly amplified. Colleagues at equal levels are in a better position to have an equitable relationship based on mutual attraction instead of a transaction relationship based on 'utilitarian' goals, as Ariani and colleagues (2011) described it.

The problem with power imbalances in romantic relationships is that, unlike many relationships outside of work, if and when the romance ends, colleagues likely have to regularly interact and work with each other. A power imbalance amplifies the potential for one party to use this contact for retribution, retaliation or harassment. If any type of romantic relationship amongst colleagues is to be forbidden, it would be wise to have formal policies against romantic relationships where power imbalances exist. That is not to say a CEO will never develop a happy romantic relationship with a secretary, or that doctors never fall in love with their patients, but formally encouraging or allowing these types of relationships is extremely unwise.

Why are office romances so common?

Another question to consider is why, if office romances are inadvisable, are they so common? There are two major and rather simple answers to why people are attracted to each other at work.

First, the proximity or closeness of other people is a key factor in why people become attracted to each other. It's why people often fall in love with the girl or boy next door and rarely with a person in another city or country. Even with the advent of internet dating, these companies know to prioritize potential mates by geographical proximity. Proximity is an important factor for friendships as well as romances. People like, love and lust after those on the same floor more often than those in other parts of the same building. Those in the same building tend to be more desirable than those at other locations. This proximity gives way to a host of other contributing factors. It's easier to get to know, understand, like and love those people with whom one interacts more frequently. Familiarity may breed contempt at times, but it is more likely to lead to more intimate ends.

The second, important, factor is the similarity of values and attitudes between people. People who are relatively evenly matched in social status, physical appearance, personality and career achievement tend to be more attracted to each other (Greenwood, Guner and Kocharkov, 2014). Studies of long-term attraction and coupling show that similarities in factors like values, education, age and a host of other factors are highly related to successful, happy, long-term romantic relationships. Work environments often bring people of similar earnings, interests, values, and with shared experience together in close quarters.

When lots of people with shared values are pulled into close quarters with a common purpose it should be unsurprising that romantic attractions arise.

Three factors to consider

If office romances are inevitable – and we would argue that they are – what's to be done? Some would say that intimate relationships between colleagues are inappropriate, unprofessional or inadvisable. They are not all wrong. While there are benefits to strong, positive relationships in the workplace, the consequences of failed office relationships can be severe. Revenge and retribution aside, there can be time wasted with importunate or scandalous encounters in the copy room. Or energy can be wasted on keeping the whole affair secret, becoming counterproductive and inefficient. There are three important considerations.

First, company policies should consider office romances, but in a measured and mature way. Some organizations will find office romances to be strictly off limits. Prison guards should, in no way and for no reason, have romantic liaisons with the prisoners. But a bit of rumpy pumpy between librarians is not the end of the world – as long as they don't make too much noise. The less appropriate romantic relationships are within the corporate culture, the more difficulties ensue.

The second matter of importance is how good the relationship is. A strong, healthy, fair romantic relationship between colleagues can improve morale and make the workplace a more pleasant place to be. Putting pressure or stress on the relationship makes things difficult for the individuals involved.

Third is the matter of power imbalances and the discontent that can result from other workers outside of the relationship. When romantic relationships result in favouritism, or unfair advantage, others will naturally and rightly feel demoralized and mistreated. Nepotism is easily recognized by others in the organization and can lead to the majority of employees becoming alienated. It can also create a great deal of resentment toward those who benefit from favoritism.

Conclusions

Romantic relationships will continue to blossom between co-workers, and there is nothing companies can do to stop that. Draconian rules often lead to gossip, slander, rumours and secrecy. Corporate policy cannot eliminate romantic entanglements from the workplace. Open and adult policies can acknowledge that romantic relationships happen, and define which are acceptable and which are inappropriate. Employers cannot ensure relationships are happy, but should explicitly prohibit exploitative sexual relationships, draw a hard line against workplace harassment, and make it clear that using power imbalances to pursue romance will not be tolerated.

References

Ariani, M G, Ebrahimi, S S and Saeedi, A (2011) Managing workplace romance; a headache for human resource leaders, *International Proceedings of Economics Development and Research*, 19

Greenwood, J, Guner, N and Kocharkov, G S (2014) Marry your like: assortative mating and income inequality, *The American Economic Review*, 104 (5)

Pierce, C A and Aguinis, H (1997) Bridging the gap between romantic relationships and sexual harassment in organizations, *Journal of Organizational Behavior*, **18**, pp 197–200

Pierce, C A and Aguinis, H (2003) Romantic relationships in organizations: a test of model formation and impact factors, *Management Research*, **1** (2), pp 161–69

Pierce, C A, Karl, K A and Brey, E T (2012) Role of workplace romance policies and procedures on job pursuit intentions, *Journal of Managerial Psychology*, **27** (3), pp 237–63

Rosenfeld, M J and Thomas, R J (2012) Searching for a mate: the rise of the internet as a social intermediary, *American Sociological Review*, **77** (4), pp 523–47

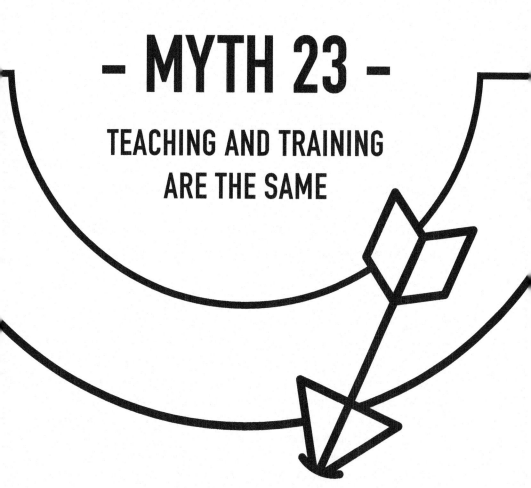

- MYTH 23 -

TEACHING AND TRAINING ARE THE SAME

The inexperienced manager may react differently under pressure than they should. But training, practice and experience help one to learn how to react and make better decisions in the future.

Introduction

Some managers take the view that training and teaching are essentially the same thing. With this approach, training would essentially be passing along knowledge, and all the training material should be available in a textbook or field manual. However, the two should not be confused. There is a stark difference and it is useful to consider both their definitions.

Teach:

- (with object and infinitive or clause) impart knowledge to or instruct (someone) as to how to do something;
- (with object) give information about or instruction in (a subject or skill).

Train:

- teach (a person or animal) a particular skill or type of behaviour through sustained practice and instruction;
- (no object) be taught through sustained practice and instruction;
- (usually as adjective trained) develop and improve (a mental or physical faculty) through instruction or practice.

The main difference is that training involves practical application of skills, typically through practice. The difference is in the spirit and intention of the activity. Teaching is more theoretical and abstract. For example, teaching in a school or university setting often involves explaining and memorizing theory and concepts without necessarily applying them. The teachers want their students to learn and understand the concepts and the background knowledge, which helps understanding.

That's not to say a more abstract approach to teaching is necessarily a problem, it's just that teaching often has a different intention than training. Knowledge and understanding about a topic can be an excellent and useful precursor to training, and in some cases that knowledge can be applied to many different areas. For example, learning about mathematics may seem an abstract (and unpleasant for some) task in school. But it is useful later in almost all aspects of work, from budgets, sales and accounts, wages and bonuses to splitting the bill and tipping at a meal with colleagues. But the distinction between teaching and training is important.

A brief note for clarification

Some would argue that good teaching involves practical components, and teachers often use applied exercises to improve their students' learning. For the purposes of this chapter we're going to use 'teaching' to refer to more abstract methods and 'training' to refer to more practical approaches. That's not to say that the two methods cannot or are not blended, but the point we're making in this chapter will be about the importance of practical, applied training in the workplace. Teaching and training may very well have a certain amount of overlap, but the gap between the two does remain large in many instances.

Differences between teaching and training

In the workplace, training tends to be quite hands-on and applied. Employees, for example, may learn some theory in college or university, but on-the-job learning happens from working with other people and practising the skills. Every experienced manager will know that business theories, theoretical models and background knowledge can be quickly abandoned in the realities and complexities of the workplace. The same is true for most types of work. In sales, for example, a scripted sales pitch can be helpful, but it only has limited usefulness when trying to sell to many different types of people.

Teaching students and employees is valuable because it involves teaching concepts that can be generally useful in any workplace, but are not necessarily focused on a specific organization. Lawyers, dentists, psychologists or accountants are taught general subjects knowing that there are a range of different types of practice they could eventually end up in. Politicians tend to go onto courses like philosophy, politics and economics even if they do end up going into fundamentally different parties with different ideas and ways of doing things. Abstract concepts like business or economics theories tend to be useful when they are more generalizable and can be used in many different settings.

A major difference between teaching and training is that the timeframe and viewpoint are very different. Academics like to think they take a longer-term view of things and do not like to be rushed. Many academics resist tight deadlines that might be expected in the workplace, and tend to be more tolerant when their students fail to meet deadlines when the consequences are less severe than in the workplace. A student's essay or project that is a week late may be a minor inconvenience while in the workplace being a week late can have extremely negative consequences. Late delivery of products or services often costs the company money. A missed deadline on a proposal will likely eliminate the company from the running. In a hospital, a delay of weeks or even hours can be the difference between life and death. So training needs to incorporate the practicalities and peculiarities of the work.

Another important difference is that students are expected to be relatively self-motivated and independent. They are provided with facilities and

Table 23.1   Differences between teaching and training

	Teaching students	Training managers
Philosophy	Theoretical/abstract	Practical/concrete
Aim	Understanding	Doing
Context	Independent	Specific
Timeframe	Long term, unlimited	Short term, immediate
Resources	Self-initiated	Provided
Tone	Critical/skeptical	Enthusiastic/zealous
Medium	Verbal/process	Diagrammatic/models
Values	Content	Style

resources like computers and libraries, software, advisors and reading lists. But it is generally up to the person to decide how much time, effort and work they put into their training. That may be a feature of some workplaces, but generally at work, people are monitored for performance, and are required to be in the office at certain times and to perform to a certain level. Students who are paying for their place at many universities are allowed to consistently fail, even when they do not put in the effort. At work, employees who consistently fail or underperform cost money and are a liability.

Teaching is typically a verbal process that requires the students to do reading or research in their own time. It is about passing on knowledge that (hopefully!) can be used at another time and for other endeavours. That's not to suggest that theories and diagrams and abstract models are not useful; they are helpful to illustrate points and improve understanding. They may, however, be less useful in a practical workplace setting under time constraints and budget limitations. Academics try to understand underlying processes or mechanisms and find ways to explain them. But those theories may not always seem directly applicable to specific situations occurring at work that are impossible to predict.

The benefits of training

Corporate trainers tend to be a bit flashier than academics. The glossy pamphlet, a clever catchphrase and attractive training materials are more appealing and tend to sell better than a textbook. Corporate trainers tend to provide well-designed and visually appealing presentations and imagery along with simple explanations for complex issues – and they like them because their clients tend to be attracted to them. Many people are wary of corporate training because some 'trainers' use a slick sales pitch to distract their clients from the fact that there is no substance or real value in the training. This is why it is essential to distinguish the content of the training from the appearance. And having that background knowledge from being taught can be a huge asset.

Skeptical teachers often criticize practical types of training when they see the training as all style and no substance. This should not be used as a cynical criticism of all training, but it emphasizes the importance of getting a good trainer with strong content. Some Americans might sum this up satisfyingly as 'all hat and no cattle'. Some academics are envious of trainers that demand high fees, but have the opposite problem of having a great deal of substance without very much style. A dry lecture with a set of stale PowerPoint notes and monotonous delivery has little appeal. One of the important things to remember about training is that when it is memorable and enjoyable the trainees remember more and become more engaged. Content that may very well be brilliant can be forgotten if the trainer has an unsophisticated or uninteresting presentation style. Style and substance are both important – but only when they come together.

Good training is valuable when it brings what people have been taught to life in the real world. For some jobs like pilots and firefighters, many drills and simulations are practised to train people to react when things go wrong. In most types of work, when people panic and are unprepared, they forget everything that they have been taught. Knowing what to do in an emergency is a very different beast than actually doing the right thing in an emergency. But practice and training teaches those involved how they *would* react, and how they *should* react.

The same is true of most work. Managers, for example, will encounter many different situations which teaching would not have sufficiently prepared them for. Inter-office conflict or performance issues of their employees will manifest in many different forms. The inexperienced manager may react differently under pressure than they should. But training, practice and experience help one to learn how to react and make better decisions in the future.

Conclusion

There will be some people who argue there is no distinction between teaching and training. Some will argue that the best teaching involves the practical components we have ascribed to training (and they would be correct). But defining them differently is a useful place to start when discussing the difference between abstract and applied learning.

There is still a gulf between the two, and in many cases the distinction is made to argue that one or the other is better. Academics like to argue that 'practical' training misses the bigger picture or would say that it's not 'grounded in theory'. Trainers in workplaces may argue that the academics don't understand the realities of the workplace, and theory does not always translate into action. Both arguments have a strong whiff of truth. But teaching and training are both valuable. They are different tools that are useful for different purposes – neither should be discarded.

Further reading

MacRae, I and Furnham, A (2014). *High Potential: How to spot, manage and develop people at work*, Bloomsbury, London

Pollice, G (2003) Teaching vs Training, IBM developerWorks. Available at: https://www.ibm.com/developerworks/rational/library/3810.html

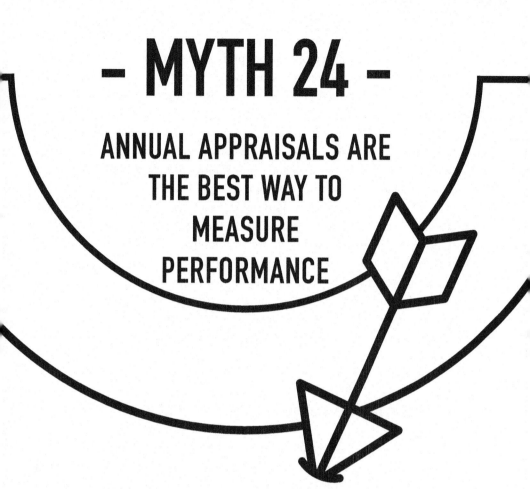

– MYTH 24 –

ANNUAL APPRAISALS ARE THE BEST WAY TO MEASURE PERFORMANCE

The annual performance review can be a useful tool when it is done well, but it's just not enough.

Introduction

The annual appraisal is an HR staple. It can also be called a performance review or performance appraisal. Sometimes it's smugly rebranded as a 'career development discussion'. Once a year, management or HR conducts a thorough review of a person's performance over the course of that year. Often it is used as a reason to talk about the person's future as well as their past performance.

It is a useful tool for discussing performance expectations, and any problems or difficulties the person being appraised might be having. It helps most employees to have a degree of certainty and regularity in their work; if they understand the expected performance and work outcomes, they are better able to meet those expectations.

It's also a good chance to set short-term as well as longer-term goals for the next year or more. Perhaps there are conversations to be had about the person's career ambitions and opportunities to take part in placements, stretch assignments or other development opportunities.

Annual appraisals are a useful way to measure performance, and certainly there is no reason to abandon them entirely (assuming they are done well). But annual appraisals are far too infrequent to properly measure performance. It is unrealistic to try to sum up an entire year's events and performance into a 30- or 60-minute interview.

First let's unpick the assumption that performance reviews are done well, and see how they can go wrong. Then we'll give some tips on how to evaluate performance well, and look at a few ways that the performance review process can be improved.

Performance reviews vs inspections

When performance management is done well it can be a huge boon to the company. Well-managed and effectively motivated employees are happier, more productive, and better workers. Bad managers are at best demotivating and at worst make people resent the organization and even tempt them to become whistleblowers or saboteurs.

The performance review process should be a dialogue – a two-way conversation where both parties have an opportunity to talk openly and honestly. When a performance review is a top-down affair where the manager or HR person instructs and the employee only listens, it is not a performance review, it's more like an inspection.

In *Motivation and Performance: A guide to motivating a diverse workforce*, MacRae and Furnham (2017) compare these types of appraisals to Politburo-style inspections. The employee is expected to be a paragon of virtue, and is paraded past the dear leader, expected to smile and talk about how great everything is. This isn't just poor practice for a performance review, it is actively damaging and an opportunity missed.

First it can be damaging to employee morale. Instead of using it to talk about performance, the work, challenges and opportunities, it becomes more like a talent show. Employees will be on their best behaviour for a few days or weeks before the annual performance review.

The second problem is that it is a missed opportunity for the managers, HR department or whoever is conducting the performance review to get some insight into the real problems in the workplace and what is going well. It's a missed opportunity for a real two-way conversation. The performance review should be approached as an opportunity to talk about the employee's performance in addition to being a great way to get some insight into what's going on in an office, department or team. What's going well? What could still be improved that might not be visible from the bird's-eye view of the leadership perspective? The value of getting this employee insight should not be underestimated.

The benefits should be apparent, but that does not mean it's easy to do. To get honest responses, the employee needs to know that the person conducting the review actually cares to listen, and will treat the information with appropriate tact and confidentiality. And the evaluators need to be able to follow up on the issues raised and be genuine about what they can and will do. People quickly become disillusioned and mistrustful when promises are not kept.

Consider a (true) example of an ex-CEO and president of a large financial institution who used to make site visits with selected members of his senior leadership team every week. These were not inspections of Potemkin villages, but were done out of genuine interest and the knowledge that in a large company, the CEO won't see everything, so it's useful to hear from employees with different perspectives. He would speak individually with some employees at the location, whether it was a department in the corporate office or a local branch. This was not an empty gesture, but came with a guarantee backed by a financial incentive. Let me know what opportunities we're missing or how we can make things better or save costs. If we use your idea and it works, you get a share of the added profits or cost sharing.

There are all sorts of ways that the management and leadership can effectively monitor performance.

Performance reviews and check-ups

The annual performance review can be a useful tool when it is done well, but it's just not enough. The yearly review will be far too infrequent to catch most of the performance issues that will crop up. It won't accurately or fully capture the employee's performance because performance can vary greatly over the course of an entire year.

One way to deal with this is to make the performance review more frequent. Semi-annual or even quarterly reviews can help to more accurately reflect performance. Of course, this can create a greater administrative burden and add to the ever-increasing amount of paperwork for HR. Some organizations combat this by having a comprehensive annual performance review, with a few check-ups on performance that are far briefer and more efficient.

Of course, documentation is an important part of the performance review. But making the documentation very brief can also help to minimize some of the burden. Computer software too can simplify the process, automate the organization and help to store and analyse the information.

There is a role for more informal check-ups and conversations. MacRae and Furnham (2017) provide an example of the manager in a small office of about 20 people. She would use a part of every morning to go around the office and have a quick chat with some of the employees. It was just a few minutes' worth of chats; a few questions about how everything was going, what are you working on today, how's your spouse doing, etc. It was a mini performance check-in almost disguised as pleasant small talk.

This type of check-up may not be feasible everywhere, but it can be adapted in various ways to different organizations. Some smart HR workers know the proverbial water cooler or break room is a great way to get information casually and informally. Some people get intimidated more by official performance reviews than by a nice quick chat.

That is not to say an informal check-in is a replacement for a well-executed, regular performance review process. It is supplemental and complementary. It can help identify day-to-day performance issues and notice any problems early, before they escalate. It also reinforces that the manager or leader is open and interested on a day-to-day basis, not just during bonus season.

We have repeatedly mentioned that regular performance appraisals are useful when they are done well. When they are done poorly they are at best a waste of resources and at worst can reduce productivity. Here are seven important points to improve the quality of the performance reviews. After this section, we offer advice for those on the receiving end of performance reviews.

Seven points about measurement and performance appraisal systems

1 **Not everyone can do them well.** Inexperienced, worried or weak managers may not give people low marks. Performance reviews can be very

difficult situations, particularly when there are performance issues. If everyone gets a mark of 4 or 5 out of 5, that is not very useful information about performance. If the scale stretches from 1 to 5 then the full scale needs to be used in evaluations and it needs to accurately reflect employee performance.

2 **Performance data should be linked to rewards.** Pay, perks or bonuses should have a clear link with the performance criteria. Day-to-day feedback may not be explicitly linked to rewards, but in the bigger picture there should be some clear performance objectives that define who gets rewarded, for what, and how.

3 **Employees should have input or involvement.** Sometimes it's challenging to get the balance right between consulting employees enough and badgering them for too much feedback. But when employees feel like the performance review criteria are irrelevant to their job or that they are isolated from the process it makes the process less useful. It can sometimes be difficult to compare performance between departments or roles, so if teams can help come up with their own criteria for what is optimal performance it gets them more involved and can provide useful insight.

4 **Combine regular feedback with structured appraisals.** As mentioned previously, both yearly appraisals and more informal day-to-day feedback can be useful. Yearly reviews can encourage people to be on their best behaviour only when the performance review is looming. The big-picture issues can be saved for the annual or semi-annual performance reviews, while the day to-day-checkups can deal with performance issues efficiently when they pop up.

5 **The rules must apply to everyone.** If certain groups receive rigorous performance reviews while other groups like management are exempt it can create a sense of unfairness and bias. Every group must have some level of involvement with the performance review system with rewards and benefits that are clearly linked to the optimal criteria in their role. Performance criteria can be flexible depending on the role but they must apply to everyone in the organization.

6 **Consider group performance as well as individual performance.** If a performance management system focuses exclusively on individual performance it can be detrimental to overall team performance. The performance review process should focus on individual and team performance, ideally with rewards that are fairly tied to both. Focus on rewarding the behaviour that is to be encouraged.

7 Rating scales should be clearly defined and standardized. The numbers used in rating performance should be clearly linked with words and/or definitions that define the level or type of performance. Performance scales should use words like 1 = Unsatisfactory performance, 2 = Satisfactory but needs improvement, 3 = Satisfactory, 4 = Above average, 5 = Excellent performance. Every evaluator needs to have the same idea about what these mean, with clear cut-off points. Define which number represents the cut-off between acceptable and unacceptable performance.

There is always a cost–benefit analysis to consider with performance reviews. Their frequency and comprehensiveness will probably have budgetary constraints. Regular, informal checkups are time-consuming and may not always seem like a priority. But consider the cost of getting it wrong.

Performance management, like measurement in general, is only useful and effective when it is done well. When it is done poorly it wastes money and demotivates the people whose very performance it should be designed to improve. When it's done right it can be a huge asset to the organization.

Advice for employees to get the most from performance appraisals

It's not just managers or HR professionals who need to make the most of performance appraisals. The responsibility falls equally on those on the receiving end of the performance review. Employees should be prepared and ready to provide the most effective information during their performance review, and consider how they can benefit from it. Here are four recommendations for those on the receiving end.

1 Keep your own career goals in mind. When performance reviews are done well, they should be mutually beneficial for the reviewer and the person being reviewed. Typically, the reviewer will have a set of performance criteria and desirable behaviour in mind. These will be more flexible or open-ended in some organizations and less so in others.

Employers, managers and HR professionals should know what they want from the employees and what performance they are attempting to measure. Yet they may be less able or less thoughtful about the employee. Work to meet the performance standards, while going into the review knowing your own skills and career goals and prepared to explain and discuss them.

2 **Find value.** Performance reviews can seem tedious, pointless or formulaic. Not all employers do performance reviews well. However, like most work situations, it is what you make of it. By following the other points of advice, being prepared and keeping your own career goals in mind you can bring more into the performance review and (ideally) get more out of it.

Even if the performance appraisal is unfocused or poorly structured, take this as an opportunity to discuss the best components of your own performance and what you do well. Perhaps it is possible to define some of your own performance appraisal criteria and highlight your own strengths in the work.

3 **Be prepared.** Go into the appraisal after considering your own performance over the full period of time the review covers. Keep notes about your own performance at work, and perhaps highlight pieces of work or projects you have done particularly well. Even if your appraiser is not prepared, use that opportunity to focus on the best work you have done.

Treat a performance appraisal the same way you would treat a job interview. Be prepared to highlight your achievements and discuss your career goals. If you have any concerns or grievances be ready to discuss them in a constructive way. If you do have problems to raise, consider what solutions there might be, or what the desirable outcome is for you. Along with highlighting your achievements, being well prepared always sends encouraging signals to appraisers.

4 **Be proactive about receiving feedback.** Not all employers are proactive or timely about performance appraisals. If you are due for one, it might be useful to politely remind the relevant manager or appraiser that it's nearly time for your appraisal and help to schedule it.

If your performance is good and you have career goals in mind, there may be more for you to lose by missing out on performance appraisals. They can be a good opportunity to discuss your performance and career goals. It's an opportunity that should not be missed.

Conclusion

It's difficult to say that annual appraisals are the best method, but this chapter has not argued that they are not good. For years, HR circles have been discussing whether or not the annual appraisal should be a thing of the past (Mitchell, 2014; Rushmore, 2017).

We would argue annual appraisals still have their usefulness, although they could use a bit of sprucing up. It's not time to ditch the annual performance review, but it is time to add some complementary methods to maximize its usefulness.

References and further reading

MacRae, and Furnham, A (2014) *High Potential: How to spot, manage and develop talented people at work*, Bloomsbury, London

MacRae, I and Furnham, A (2017) *Motivation and Performance: A guide to motivating a diverse workforce*, Kogan Page, London

Mitchell, L (2014) Are annual appraisals losing impact? *HR Magazine*, 25 November. Available at: http://www.hrmagazine.co.uk/article-details/are-annual-appraisals-losing-impact

Rushmore, K (2017) Annual appraisals – good, bad or just ugly? *Personnel Today*, 1 February. Available at: http://www.personneltoday.com/hr/annual-appraisals-good-bad-just-ugly/

– MYTH 25 –

HIGH ACHIEVERS ALWAYS MAKE GREAT MANAGERS

*There is no guarantee that a top performer in any particular
job will naturally be a good manager or leader.*

Introduction

A common workplace myth embedded in much of the practice of human
resource departments is that the top-performing employee is the best candidate for a managerial or leadership role. There is much interest in what
makes a high flyer so successful, from ambitious employees and selectors
alike. There are many different theories about what makes people successful; many have the underlying assumption that high performance in one role
will translate into equivalent performance in another role.

It is common in most workplaces and types of jobs that a high-performing employee is promoted from a role of expertise or specialism into a managerial or leadership role. The problem here can be described as the *Performance Delusion* (MacRae and Furnham, 2014, 2017). It is a mistake that occurs when promoting an employee assuming that specialist or technical skills in a role will naturally translate into a completely different skill set such as leadership. This is a persistent problem in the workplace, particularly for human resources.

Those who have practised or trained for a particular job can spend a great deal of time and energy mastering skills. These may or may not be skills that are transferrable to leadership. The highest-performing nurse is not guaranteed to be the best nurse manager; the most successful teacher has no guarantee of being the best head teacher. Leadership career trajectories are fundamentally a different type of job than mastering a particular role (MacRae and Furnham, 2014). It is a common myth that the top performer in one type of work should be rewarded with a promotion to a leadership position. But without proper development of skills and training, this can be a quick path to demotivation, derailment and failure.

Peter and Hull (1994) describe the 'Peter Principle', that competent people tend to get promoted until they rise to a level beyond their capability. 'Work is accomplished by those employees who have not yet reached their level of incompetence' (Peter and Hull, 1994).

This is a problem that frequently occurs in all types of work, but in specialized jobs in particular. The person may be competent, motivated and skilled at a particular type of work. This is why it is essential to make the distinction between mastery and leadership skill at work.

Leadership vs mastery

It is possible to distinguish between two fundamentally different types of career trajectories. **Mastery** career paths involve becoming a specialist or expert in a particular field. Lawyers and physicians spend a lifetime 'practising' in their profession. Engineers and technicians can spend an entire career span becoming better engineers and technicians. They develop their skills and knowledge and gain experience of how to do their job even better.

Leadership career paths are fundamentally different because they involve managing others, influencing them and building relationships. Although mastery skills can be useful in managing and leading others, the leader rarely or never uses these skills. Good technicians can make terrible managers

Table 25.1 Leadership vs mastery

Mastery	Leadership
Mastery means doing the specific job well. 'Key factors include: ... a highly developed knowledge base founded on extensive and varied experience that is grounded in occupation; and a set of essential behaviours, actions and processes.' (Burke and DePoy, 1991)	*Leadership requires 'doing relationships' well.* 'Leadership involves not only an individual, but an individual's exercise of influence over others.' (Burke and DePoy, 1991)

when they do not have the leadership skills, experience or ability. Promoting the top-performing technician can often result in losing the best technician and getting a bad manager (MacRae and Furnham, 2014).

The problem arises when career success is portrayed as a ladder, with a managerial position as the implicit reward for top performance. But if someone is good at their job and enjoys it, do they really want to spend the rest of their career watching others do that job? The box below explains the difference between mastery and leadership types of focus. It is essential to make the distinction between the two, particularly when asking the question about whether or not high achievers can make great managers. Realistically, high performers may have the potential to make great managers or leaders, but they will likely need to develop an entire new set of skills.

The question really must be, what can be used to identify potential managers? The answer is it essentially requires three factors: ability, motivation and reputation. All three are necessary in varying doses depending on the organization and level of seniority.

Ability

The specific type of **ability** varies depending on the company and occupational sector, but it is clear that ability to do the job well is an essential component. In leadership this means possessing or developing the appropriate leadership skills, people skills and relationship management. It requires 'managing up' – working well with more senior leadership – as well as 'managing down' – working well with direct reports. Intelligence is an asset. More complex and demanding types of work require greater levels of intelligence, but it would not be unfair to observe that management and intelligence do not always go hand in hand. Sometimes charming, confident and dense appears to be enough to win a promotion.

Motivation

The next requirement is a factor those hard-of-thinking managers neglect or ignore: **motivation**. There are two questions to ask, about the level of motivation as well as the direction. It is necessary that the person is motivated, ambitious and they want to be an effective leader. But the more neglected question is, *motivated to do what?* Does the IT specialist, accountant or nurse actually want to become a manager? If they are motivated to use their front-line expertise, a management role might be profoundly demotivating. If the person is motivated to become a leader, ask why. For those motivated by money, power or influence, independence or benevolence, their motivation can greatly affect their performance. Never underestimate the importance of motivation as a factor in success. Without motivation, the greatest ability can flounder or fail.

Reputation

The third factor, unlike intelligence, can be built and developed. However, it is a difficult beast to tame and is not entirely under one's own control: **reputation**. Successful leaders understand the importance of developing, maintaining and improving relationships and managing their reputation. Those who gain a reputation for being fair, ethical, hardworking and good at their job can rely on their reputation to influence others around them. Those that have a reputation for being thin-skinned, aggressive and unforgiving may use that reputation in different ways. Marketing and communications types are often accused of focusing on developing reputation with only a minor wisp of truth. The less emotionally intelligent workers ignore their reputation at work at their peril and often to their detriment. But when there is a large gap between a manager's reputation and their actual behaviour in the workplace, reputation is harmed. Reputation is important, but the ideal reputation varies greatly depending on the organization and situation.

> You do not lead by hitting people over the head – that's assault, not leadership.
> (Dwight Eisenhower)

Having just one or two of the three factors above is simply not enough. Lack of ability will lead quickly to failure. Without motivation, nothing will happen. And a terrible reputation can quickly destroy what could have been an otherwise promising career. Titles like 'disgraced former MP' can follow someone for a lifetime. The following case study is a prime example of how badly things can go wrong when the wrong people lead a company.

CASE STUDY An example of leadership derailment

Between 1985 and 2001, Enron had a spectacular rise and equally spectacular and rapid collapse. One of the main reasons for the company's failure is often attributed to leadership failure. Although the leaders were extraordinarily intelligent and talented, which contributed to the company's initial success, intelligence alone also became a problem. In the aftermath, commentators generally agreed that Enron's leaders were fantastically intelligent but also ill-suited to run the company.

They managed to create an illusion of company success that relied on some very creative accounting measures which made them appear much more successful than they actually were. They created a complex system arranged to hide a vast amount of debt and inflate their profits. It all unravelled in 2001 when they posted a loss of US $618 million and a US Securities and Exchange Commission found financial fraud on a massive scale. This is a great example of the Peter Principle and the Performance Delusion in action. The company may have had some fantastically motivated people who would do anything to make the company appear successful and make a great deal of money out of it. But despite being highly skilled, intelligent and motivated, in the end there were severe problems with the leadership, which was implicated in the inevitable and swift demise of the company.

For a brief period of time, Enron appeared to be one of the largest companies in the world. Investors (many of whom were employees) lost billions of dollars as the share price plummeted from $90 to under $1. Five thousand employees lost their jobs and many also lost pensions, while Enron executives had been paying themselves massive bonuses for years.

Enron is not the first case of its kind and will certainly not be the last. But the lesson is extremely clear: the costs of getting the wrong managers and leaders can be dire. It is essential that managers and leaders have the proper skills, knowledge and abilities to lead successfully.

Conclusion

There is no guarantee that a top performer in any particular job will naturally be a good manager or leader. That doesn't mean a good technician or expert cannot or will not be able to learn to be a great leader – many can and do. They need appropriate development and training opportunities to build, develop and master the new skills.

Similarly, it should not be assumed that a top performer naturally wants to move from a specialist role into a leadership role. Often derailment occurs at work when taking a top-performing employee away from the job they enjoy and do well, and putting them into a managerial role. They are taken away from their expertise, then end up supervising others and watching them do work the new manager may prefer. High achievers may make great managers, but there is no guarantee.

References

Burke, J P and DePoy, E (1991) An emerging view of mastery, excellence, and leadership in occupational therapy practice, *American Journal of Occupational Therapy*, **45** (11) pp 1027–32

MacRae, I and Furnham, A (2014) *High Potential: How to spot, manage and develop talented people at work*, Bloomsbury, London

MacRae, I and Furnham, A (2017) *Motivation and Performance: A guide to motivating a diverse workforce*, Kogan Page, London

Peter, L J and Hull, R (1994) *The Peter Principle: Why things always go wrong*, Souvenir Press Ltd, London

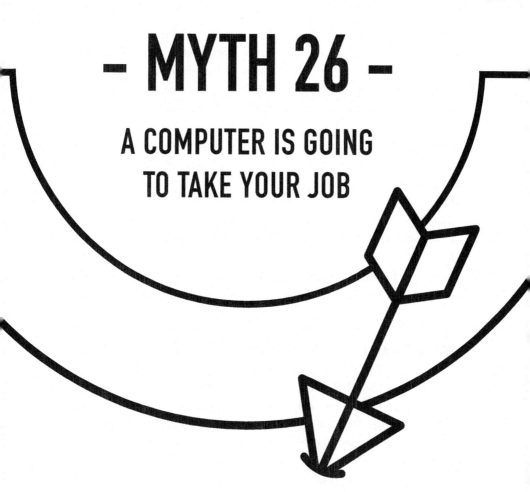

– MYTH 26 –

A COMPUTER IS GOING TO TAKE YOUR JOB

For some types of work automation is far from practical, realistic or cost-effective.

Introduction

There is a great deal of interest, excitement and concern about the effects computers and robots will have on the workplace and workforce. Computer programs can replace entire occupations, as travel agents and bank tellers have discovered very quickly and with much consternation. Dentists, religious leaders, teachers and editors have likewise noticed that their unique insight, specialized knowledge or social dexterity are much more difficult to replace with a machine.

An Oxford University study by Frey and Osborne (2013) estimated that nearly 50 per cent of jobs were under threat by computerization and automation, but they predicted stark differences in different sectors. For example, they calculated the probability of computers taking people's jobs and predicted a very high probability for telemarketers (99 per cent), accountants and auditors (94 per cent) and retail salespeople (92 per cent). The lowest probability was for recreational therapists (0.0 per cent), dentists (0.7 per cent), athletic trainers (0.7 per cent) and clergy (0.8 per cent). It's easy to imagine Apple or Android developing accounting or shopping apps. It is much more difficult to imagine the Apple iNun or a Google ToothXtract.me becoming overnight successes.

This is one myth that is impossible to answer without looking into more detail about the particular job and sector. For some types of work, automation is far from practical, realistic or cost-effective. Other jobs have automation looming on the horizon, if not already underway.

Jobs that can be replaced by a computer

A report by the MIT *Technology Review* (Rotman, 2013) suggests that people's jobs have been being replaced by machines for at least 300 years, since the industrial revolution. Manual jobs continuously turn into mechanical jobs where more labour can be done by fewer people, with the help of machines.

Even in the 20th century, for example, which saw massive growth of agricultural productivity in the United States, agricultural employment fell from 41 per cent of the population in 1900 to 2 per cent in the year 2000. With production in mind, this means over the course of 100 years, American farms were producing 800 per cent more output with only 5 per cent of the workforce. Figure 26.1 below shows what this means for both employment and productivity (based on statistics from Alston et al, 2010; Dmitri, Effland and Conklin, 2005). Over the course of 100 years, 1 per cent of the labour force could create 160 times more output.

Any job that is relatively routine and straightforward to automate, from jobs on the retail sales floor which can be moved online, to routine tasks such as those found in logistics, shipping and warehouses, can be automated to both increase productivity and decrease costs. A type of warehouse robot, for example, can quadruple the productivity of a warehouse when replacing its human counterparts. Robots don't have labour disputes, are not subject

Figure 26.1 Change in American agricultural output and employment

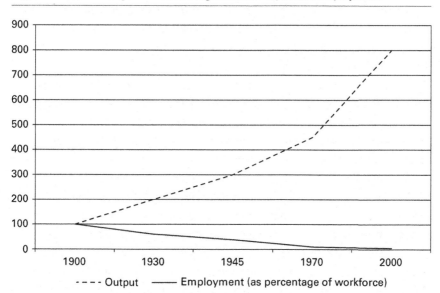

- - - - Output   —— Employment (as percentage of workforce)

to labour laws, don't need tea breaks, and don't forgot where a product is located. They are interchangeable and are easily replaced.

Lost jobs are an incredibly attractive prospect to populist politicians, who will shamelessly promise the return of thousands or millions of jobs to companies and communities that have been beleaguered by job losses, often in particular industries. The next case study illustrates how jobs lost to automation can be impossible or inconceivable to get back.

CASE STUDY Automation

Professor Lawrence Katz, economics professor at Harvard University, sees automation as a revolution in the labour market, which could all but destroy traditional factory production jobs (Thompson, 2015). Working-class steel belts, areas of well-paid, blue-collar, aspirational Americans in the middle of the 20th century are collapsing in on themselves and while some politicians may have blamed foreign governments, international trade policy or external factors, Professor Katz states the cause as, 'Over the long haul, clearly automation's been much more important – it's not even close' (Miller, 2016).

Like agriculture, the American steel industry has seen a steep decline in employment, without a corresponding decline in productivity. Between 1962 and

2005 the American steel industry lost about 75 per cent of its workforce, while maintaining the same level of production, according to a study in the *American Economic Review* (Collard-Wexler and De Loecker, 2015). This means that when an industry becomes four times more productive, only a quarter of the workers are required to fulfil demand.

Automation does have the effect of killing some jobs and creating new ones, but the new jobs are rarely aligned with the job losses. Manual, production or lower-skilled jobs tend to be replaced with highly technical or specialized jobs. They are jobs of the future but are often not jobs for the people who have lost employment due to automation or computerization.

Miller (2016) recounts the stories of many workers in American steel-producing swing states like Indiana, who lost high-paying manufacturing jobs, falling into tenuous, lower-paid and part-time employment. The consequences of automation are an open secret and show no signs of stopping. In a show of political grandstanding, US President Trump made a show of preserving American production with HVAC manufacturer, Carrier Systems. The promise: US government investment in the company in exchange for the promise that no American jobs would be outsourced to Mexico. The CEO of the company quickly agreed to the deal, but said that the investment money would be spent on automation and that 'What that ultimately means is there will be fewer jobs' (as cited in Miller, 2016).

Jobs which are difficult to automate

Many jobs are on the frontline of automation, with jobs likely to be lost to computers within the coming months, years, and decades. Other jobs are much safer because they are much more difficult for a computer or robot to do. The risks are by no means shared equally between occupations or work sectors.

Frey and Osborne (2013) outline types of work that computers are unlikely to replace in the next few decades.

- **Creative intelligence tasks.** Any jobs which require the person to come up with interesting, unique or novel ideas are difficult to automate or computerize; tasks which have clear, consistent and reliable steps or actions, by definition, can be automated. If the process is straightforward and already known, a computer can be programmed to do it. If the outcome is largely unknown and requires a creative or new solution, then it is extraordinarily difficult to automate. A computer may be able to generate outcomes that are 'new' – computers can easily generate images that have never before been created – but they create newness in the sense of randomness, having a great deal of difficulty applying novel solutions to a problem they have not been programmed to address. A computer can recognize patterns and applied predefined sets of actions, but cannot 'make sense' of the situation or a solution.

- **Social intelligence tasks.** Computers can be programmed along set courses of actions or to complete discrete tasks, but are currently woefully incapable of understanding any emotions, thoughts, or working with complex and nuanced social contexts surrounding the predetermined set of actions. Computers lack the capability to use techniques of persuasion, empathy and care that are required for many different types of work that involve working with, caring for, and understanding others. Although robots may be able to create the appearance of care or understanding, by being programmed with the appropriate language output, they lack the true capability, along with the insight and creativity required to deal with these issues, as addressed in the previous point.

While there are efforts being made to help computers with creative intelligence tasks and social intelligence tasks (eg Scherer, Bänziger and Roesch, 2010; Broekens, Heerink and Rosendal, 2009), they are still a long way off. Steel workers, shop assistants, drivers and warehouse shipper/receivers should be worried about their jobs tomorrow and next year. Fashion designers, surgeons and public relations professionals can worry less about a computer taking their job.

Conclusions

While it is relatively easy to predict some of the jobs where human workers will be replaced by computers, there will be others that seem impossible to predict. It can also be difficult to predict what new jobs technology will create. Jobs like social media managers, app developers, cloud computing specialists or drone operators are relatively new. However, many of the new jobs will be related to the very same advances in automation and working with computers.

There is a great deal of truth in the idea that computers and robots can take jobs. It is inevitable that many jobs will be lost to computers or robots. For jobs that are relatively straightforward to automate, this is not a myth, while for work that requires more caring, intellect or insight, computers are a much more distant threat.

References

Alston, J M et al (2010) *Persistence Pays: US agricultural productivity growth and the benefits from public R&D spending*, Springer

Broekens, J, Heerink, M and Rosendal, H (2009) Assistive social robots in elderly care: a review, *Gerontechnology*, 8 (2), pp 94–103

Collard-Wexler, A and De Loecker, J (2015) Reallocation and technology: evidence from the US steel industry, *American Economic Review*, 105 (1), pp 131–71

Dmitri, C, Effland, A and Conklin, N (2005) The 20th-Century transformation of US agriculture and farm policy, *Economic Information Bulletin Number 3*, United States Department of Agriculture

Frey, B C and Osborne, M A (2013) The future of employment: how susceptible are jobs to computerization? Oxford Martin. Available at: http://www.oxfordmartin.ox.ac.uk/downloads/academic/The_Future_of_Employment.pdf

Miller, C C (2016) The long-term jobs killer is not China. It's automation, *New York Times*, 21 December. Available at: https://www.nytimes.com/2016/12/21/upshot/the-long-term-jobs-killer-is-not-china-its-automation.html

Rotman, D (2013) How technology is destroying jobs, *MIT Technology Review*, July/August

Scherer, K R, Bänziger, T and Roesch, E B (2010) *Blueprint for Affective Computing: A sourcebook and manual*, Oxford University Press, Oxford

Thompson, D (2015) A world without work, *The Atlantic*, 5 July. Available at: https://www.theatlantic.com/magazine/archive/2015/07/world-without-work/395294/

– MYTH 27 –

OPEN-PLAN OFFICES ARE ALWAYS THE BEST OPTION

These types of workspaces are actually making some people sicker.

Introduction

In 2015, Mark Zuckerberg, creator of Facebook, did what many CEOs had done before him – he moved his team to an open-plan office. Deep inside the new headquarters of Facebook, over 2,800 employees now work in a one-mile-long room. Facebook joins a long stream of companies who have jumped on the open-plan concept bandwagon. Over 70 per cent of offices in the United States are now free of walls and doors.

In the 1950s, modernist architects designed the open-plan office – defined as large open spaces, shared work areas, and few private offices – as a rebuttal against the monotonous work lives of employees, and knocked down walls in an attempt to get people to talk to each other and develop relationships. A cubicle system was developed by a German design team who created what's known as an 'office landscape' to put a little bit of soul back into the offices. This concept that utilized furniture and organic geometry to create an open office landscape was intended to foster innovation, productivity and new relationships.

Companies were quick to adopt this system. Was it to liberate their workers? Give them more flexibility and space? No, is the answer. It was mostly to fit as many employees as they could into one room, which results in reduced costs... *hypothetically.*

As the number of open-plan offices increased, so did the research on their effectiveness. The general consensus appears to be that these modern workspaces don't quite live up to the high expectations. Davis, Leach and Clegg (2011) reviewed over 100 studies that examined the usefulness of open-plan offices. They concluded that this form of workplace is damaging to employee satisfaction due to the increased noise levels and distractions that come with a privacy-challenged office. These are just the start of some of the issues with open-plan offices.

How the open-plan office killed productivity

An open environment compared to traditional ones fosters a louder and more disruptive atmosphere. Noise distractions are abundant within an office, be it telephones ringing, people coming in and out of the office, or your co-workers talking to you or each other. The World Health Organization (2012) reported that these noise levels result in over £30 billion loss within Europe each year – definitely not as low cost as companies initially thought!

Part of this loss includes workers taking more sick leave than they did prior to the shift to open-plan offices. That's right, these types of workspaces are actually making some people *sicker* – disease tends to spread fast when sharing an office with more than 20 people. In a comparison between Swedish employees who work in private offices and those who work in open-plan offices, Danielsson and his colleagues (2014) reported that people who work in open-plan offices were nearly twice as likely to take short-term sick leave (of one week or less) than those who worked in private offices.

While noise pollution can theoretically be solved with a pair of noise-cancelling headphones, visual pollution is harder to overcome. Myriad unavoidable distractors can come into an employee's field of vision, causing their concentration to falter and their eyes to avert their screens. On average, workers will be distracted every 11 minutes during their day (Steelcase,

2014)! This makes it (even) harder to multitask and focus, especially while reading or writing.

One size does not fit all

While open-plan offices work well for some groups of people, they don't work for everybody. There are definite generational differences when arguing which office layout is the most conducive to a better working environment. Older generations who are used to more traditional forms of working tend to be the loudest in their complaints regarding open-plan offices.

The Millennials on the other hand are more optimistic about this work layout considering they most likely haven't experienced any other way of working. Open offices may be better suited for younger workers who are more prepared for the trade-offs; many often believe the lack of privacy and greater noise levels are worth it when they are able to communicate better within their teams and friends.

This conclusion is also applicable to extroverts as well, who value casual interactions and ease of communication with their colleagues. On the other hand, open-plan offices can be detrimental to an introvert's working experience, due to their high sensitivity to external stimulation. The constant noise and visual distractions, as well as uncontrollable interactions, can result in higher levels of stress and reduced performance levels for introverts. Extroverts are more likely to benefit from the presence of these distractions (to a certain extent – even extroverts have their limits). A large body of literature supports these claims and many researchers have found introverts perform more poorly on cognitive ability tasks (eg memory tests) in the presence of background noise such as music compared to silence (Cassidy and MacDonald, 2007).

Open communication but loss of privacy

It can be argued that open-plan layouts facilitate greater communication between employees. Instead of e-mailing a fellow employee, you can simply roll your chair three feet and have a quick chat. But to what extent are these types of conversations useful and about purely work-related topics?

As intended, new and unexpected bonds are created between co-workers as a consequence of the ease of interaction that open-plan offices provide. However, in conjunction there appears to be a loss in performance levels. Greater levels of communication have been shown to damage workers' attention spans and creative thinking.

More importantly, the loss of privacy also causes performance levels to plummet as people feel a reduced sense of control and engagement in their work (Kim and Dear, 2013). Perhaps a feeling of control acts as a moderator for the office-related distractions that employees face. Or the empowerment that comes alongside control provides a strong motivator to accomplish more, faster (Lee and Brand, 2005). The latest craze of 'hot desking', where individuals are not assigned a desk but take whichever is free, does not help an employee's lack of control of their environment either.

Conclusion

While the open-plan office remains the layout of choice across the globe, its effectiveness is limited. No office plan is perfect and trade-offs will always be present – so the types of employees and the type of company must be considered when deciding on an office layout. Jobs such as writing, financial planning and other disciplines that require deep concentration should perhaps ditch the open-plan layout and stick to more traditional ways.

References

Cassidy, G and MacDonald, R A R (2007) The effect of background music and background noise on the task performance of introverts and extroverts, *Psychology of Music*, 35 (3)

Danielsson, C et al (2014) Office design's impact on sick leave rates, *Ergonomics*, 57 (2), pp 139–47

Davis, M, Leach, D J and Clegg C W (2011) The physical environment of the office: contemporary and emerging issues, *International Review of Industrial and Organizational Psychology*, 26, pp 193–235

Kim, J and Dear, R (2013) Workplace satisfaction: the privacy–communication trade-off in open-plan offices, *Journal of Environmental Psychology*, 36, pp 18–26

Lee, S and Brand, J (2005) Effects of control over office workspace on perceptions of the work environment and work outcomes, *Journal of Environmental Psychology*, 25, pp 323–33

Steelcase (2014) The privacy crisis: taking a toll on employee engagement, *Steelcase*. Available at: https://www.steelcase.com/insights/articles/privacy-crisis/

World Health Organization (2012) Burden of disease from environmental noise, WHO. Available at: http://www.euro.who.int/en/publications/abstracts/burden-of-disease-from-environmental-noise.-quantification-of-healthy-life-years-lost-in-europe

INDEX

Note: page numbers in *italic* indicate figures or tables.

CPSIA information can be obtained
at www.ICGtesting.com
Printed in the USA
BVOW06s0939031017
496581BV00005B/61/P